Praise for *Key business solut*

The most successful businesses don't avoid problems – they solve them. This practical, insightful and entertaining book guides you through how to do this. An indispensable resource for any manager.

RICHARD NEWTON, BUSINESS CONSULTANT AND BESTSELLING
AUTHOR OF *THE PROJECT MANAGER*

One of the key attributes in running a business successfully is the ability to see a situation in perspective. Too often the real issues go unrecognised, signs are misread, an opportunity slips by, the wrong problem is addressed. Only in retrospect is it obvious what should have been done.

It is not easy but the tools and techniques covered in Key Business Solutions should help.

SIR GEORGE COX, AUTHOR OF THE HM TREASURY *COX REVIEW OF CREATIVITY
IN BUSINESS* AND FORMER CHAIRMAN OF THE DESIGN COUNCIL

Antonio is a problem-solving expert and a brilliant writer. His clear thinking on the vital business skills covered in this book will transform the way you manage.

ANDREW SHELTON, INDEPENDENT CONSULTANT

The tools and techniques covered in this book will be of enormous benefit to any manager. I thoroughly recommend it.

CAROLINE CAKE, DIRECTOR, 2020 DELIVERY

Key business solutions

FT Prentice Hall
FINANCIAL TIMES

In an increasingly competitive world, we believe it's quality of thinking that gives you the edge – an idea that opens new doors, a technique that solves a problem, or an insight that simply makes sense of it all. The more you know, the smarter and faster you can go.

That's why we work with the best minds in business and finance to bring cutting-edge thinking and best learning practice to a global market.

Under a range of leading imprints, including *Financial Times Prentice Hall*, we create world-class print publications and electronic products bringing our readers knowledge, skills and understanding, which can be applied whether studying or at work.

To find out more about Pearson Education publications, or tell us about the books you'd like to find, you can visit us at **www.pearson.com/uk**

ANTONIO E. WEISS

Key business solutions

Essential problem-solving tools and techniques
that every manager needs to know

Financial Times
Prentice Hall
is an imprint of

Harlow, England • London • New York • Boston • San Francisco • Toronto • Sydney • Singapore • Hong Kong
Tokyo • Seoul • Taipei • New Delhi • Cape Town • Madrid • Mexico City • Amsterdam • Munich • Paris • Milan

PEARSON EDUCATION LIMITED

Edinburgh Gate
Harlow CM20 2JE
Tel: +44 (0)1279 623623
Fax: +44 (0)1279 431059
Website: www.pearson.com/uk

First published in Great Britain in 2011

Pearson Education is not responsible for the content of third-party internet sites.

ISBN: 978-0-273-75029-1

British Library Cataloguing-in-Publication Data
A catalogue record for this book is available from the British Library

Library of Congress Cataloging-in-Publication Data
Weiss, Antonio E.
  Key business solutions : essential problem-solving tools and techniques that every manager needs to know / Antonio E. Weiss.
      p. cm.
  Includes bibliographical references.
  ISBN 978-0-273-75029-1 (pbk.)
  1. Problem-solving. 2. Management. I. Title.
  HD30.29.W44 2011
  658.4'03--dc23
                                        2011024730

Microsoft screen shots reprinted with permission from Microsoft Corporation.

10 9 8 7 6 5 4 3 2 1
15 14 13 12 11

Typeset in 9.25pt Swiss Light by 3
Printed and bound in Great Britain by Ashford Colour Press

For my family, and especially,
my parents – a constant source
of love and inspiration.

Contents

About the author

Antonio E. Weiss is a management consultant and writer. Antonio learnt about solving tough business problems at one of the UK's leading boutique management consultancy firms, 2020 Delivery. There he has worked across a range of public sector organisations, focusing on issues varying from performance improvement and pathway redesign to efficiency savings and designing and delivering training courses on data modelling and problem-solving. On a *pro bono* basis in an independent consulting capacity he has also worked on industrial policy in Central Asia.

Antonio also likes to apply his problem-solving skills to a number of different situations outside the business world. He is a governor of one of the largest community colleges in London and has also written for a number of publications, including the *Guardian*, on a variety of issues. In between consulting and his other responsibilities, his next project is to write a history of management consultancy in Britain. He holds a Bachelor's and a Master's degree in History from the University of Cambridge.

Antonio would be interested to hear your thoughts on *Key business solutions*. You can contact him via his website: **www.antonioweiss.com**

Acknowledgements

Firstly, this book owes a deep debt and much gratitude to my friends and colleagues at 2020 Delivery, one of the UK's leading public sector consultancy firms. My thinking on business problems has been greatly influenced and shaped by 2020 Delivery's own problem-solving and process improvement methodologies. I am thankful not only for the opportunity to work with such brilliant minds at 2020 Delivery, but also for the freedom to develop that I have been given there. I will always be grateful for this.

Secondly, I would like to thank Liz Gooster of Pearson Education. Not only has she been an excellent, thoughtful and responsive editor, she also had the confidence to accept my proposal in the first place. Without her support there would be no *Key business solutions*. I am also very grateful to numerous individuals who have helped the book at various points. In particular, these are Richard Newton, Linda Dhondy, Emma Devlin, Rachel Hayter, Viv Church, Anna Jackson and Andy Sims of andysimsphotography.

Lastly, I must thank my wonderful and patient partner, Carol. My debt to her is already enormous, and no doubt, still growing.

Publisher's acknowledgements

We are grateful to the following for permission to reproduce copyright material:

Figure on page 173 adapted from 'Stratogies of diversification' *Harvard Business Review*, 25(5), 113–25m Sept–Oct (Ansoff, I. 1957); Figure on page 175 adapted from The BCG Portfolio Matrix from the Product Portflio Matrix, © 1970, The Boston Consulting Group; Figure on page 182 adapted from 'Attractive quality and must-be quality', *Hinshitsu: The Journal of the Japanese Society for Quality Control*, April, 39–48 (Kano, N., Seraku, N., Takahashi, F. and Tsuji, S. 1984); Figure on page 185 adapted from 'Structure is not organization', *Mckinsey Quarterly* (Waterman, R.H., Peters, T.J. and Phillips, J.R. 1980); Figure on page 187 adapted from 'How competitive forces shape strategy', *Harvard Business Review*, March/April (Porter, M. 1979).

In some instances we have been unable to trace the owners of copyright material, and we would appreciate any information that would enable us to do so.

Introduction

Obtain the solution to your business problems

These days it seems everyone has a problem. Turn on the television and you'll hear politicians saying we need to frame the problem then solve it. Businesspeople talk about finding solutions to their problems. Salespeople guarantee you that their product will solve all of your problems. Famously, the crew of the Apollo 13 spaceship warned: 'Houston, we have a problem.' Everyone knows what to do when they have a problem. It's simple: solve it. But very few people have a proven methodology for doing this, let alone a book that will guide them successfully through the way. This is that book.

Key business solutions is about how to solve business problems. It helps you do this in two unique ways. Firstly, it introduces my own proven problem-solving methodology – the OBTAIN process – and guides you through the tools and techniques which are used at each stage of the process (see the Appendix for an overview of the chapter contents). Through following the OBTAIN methodology you will be able to solve all of your toughest business problems. From 'What do we need to do to meet our cost reduction programmes?' to 'How can I improve my team's morale?' to 'What should the strategy be for my organisation?', the OBTAIN process can help you solve all these problems, and many more.

Secondly, *Key business solutions* is a vital reference guide for 35 of the most powerful tools and techniques commonly used in business (see the table on page xvi for a list). Each stage of the OBTAIN process uses a number of these indispensable business tools and brings them to life with detailed descriptions, explanatory examples, and tips and tricks on how to make the most of them. At the end of the book is Chapter 9 entitled *Critical business tools and frameworks* where further techniques are included. Whilst these do not fit directly into the OBTAIN process, they complement it and so are included for your benefit.

In short, *Key business solutions* is essentially two books in one: a solutions manual to guide you through solving your toughest business problems and a reference guide for some of the most powerful business tools and techniques.

What is the OBTAIN problem-solving process?

Effective problem-solving is about logical thinking based on robust analytical evidence. The OBTAIN process (see the figure opposite) takes you through a six-step methodology to help you achieve this.

- Outline. Start by framing your problem into a succinctly stated goal that you need to achieve. Once you have understood the goal you then need to get a sense of the context and history surrounding it.

The OBTAIN problem-solving process

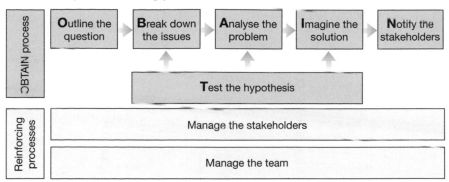

- **Break down.** Most problems are knotty and hard to untangle. By breaking down your problem to turn it into manageable chunks it becomes much easier to solve. You then need to prioritise your workload to maximise your effectiveness.

- **Test.** Problem-solving can be a time-consuming business. In order to hit the ground running, you should ensure that your thinking is always hypothesis-driven. This means that rather than collecting all the facts then coming up with a solution, you start with a hypothetical solution and then test it, discard it or refine it.

- **Analyse.** By generating robust analyses you will be able to verify your hypothesis until eventually you get to the root cause of your problem.

- **Imagine.** Solutions to business problems are often based on questionable assumptions and a weak evidence base. By ensuring your solutions – generated by a wide group of stakeholders – are grounded in robust analysis you can come up with innovative solutions that are met with the support of all your important stakeholders.

- **Notify.** Many solutions fall down due to bad communication. The tools and techniques covered in this chapter focus on compelling report writing and powerful presentations.

Two further chapters supplement the OBTAIN process:

- **Manage the stakeholders.** Here the importance of good stakeholder communication, trust, and keeping the most important stakeholder – you – happy are shown to be crucial to a successful problem-solving process.

- **Manage the team.** A happy team is a good team. By creating the right team dynamic and working on developing your team members you will ensure that your team is fully committed to solving the problem.

What are the tools and techniques covered in the book?

Thirty-five of the most important business tools and techniques are covered in *Key business solutions* (see the table overleaf).

Who is this book for?

Whilst this book is primarily for business leaders, managers at all levels, aspiring managers, management consultants and students of management, it is ultimately useful for anyone who has ever wanted to know how to solve a problem. Though the tools and techniques covered in this book are described with reference to business environments the concepts and principles inscribed in the text can be replicated in any manner of situations.

A word of warning. This book does not give you a laundry list of techniques for solving any given business problem. Rather, it gives you a methodology for how to frame, approach and solve any problem that you may come across. How you use and adapt the OBTAIN framework will inevitably be dependent on the nature of the problem; in other words, the problem should drive the process, not the other way around. This book is there to support you, guide you, and help you implement the OBTAIN problem-solving methodology and its various tools and techniques. But you are still the key ingredient that will determine the success of the problem-solving process. You must bring your own instincts, insights and personality to the problem-solving journey. I hope you enjoy doing so.

How should this book be read?

This book serves two purposes: to act as both a problem-solving manual and a reference guide for key business tools and techniques. To be used in the first way, it should be read in a linear fashion, referring to relevant chapters and sections where signposted in the text. For use as a reference guide, it can be dipped in and out of as you please. In the latter case, the table (above) is a useful map of where various tools can be found.

A note on the examples

Each chapter contains examples (many based on case studies) describing how and when you would use a particular tool or technique. All of the examples are fictional. They are there to illustrate how the tools and techniques function. Whilst the constraints of time and space mean the examples will inevitably simplify certain issues, it is intended that they provide you with a better (and hopefully entertaining) understanding of the principles behind the tools and techniques covered.

[PART ONE]

The OBTAIN problem-solving process

Outline the question

1

The OBTAIN problem-solving process

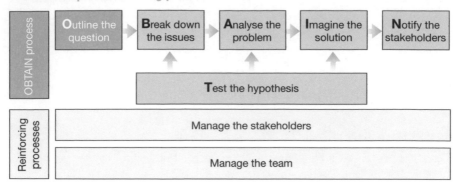

1.1 The problem may be big, but it should fit on one page

> **Key tool:**
> - **Problem statement**
>
> **Fundamental principle:**
> All the vital issues you and your stakeholders need to know stated on one page.

What is a problem statement?

Do you ever feel unsure of exactly what you are supposed to be working on? Perhaps you have a general idea of the goal your team is trying to reach, but no idea of when you are supposed to reach it by – or even how you will know if you have reached it? Or maybe you have a clear set of goals, objectives, and deadlines for a piece of work, only for your boss to change his mind at the last minute and pile a whole load of extra demands on you, completely changing the focus of your work?

These issues arise due to a lack of definition when trying to solve a business problem. They need to be confronted head-on and prevented from happening right at the start of a piece of work. This is where you need a *problem statement* (see Figure 1.1).

Problems statements are important because they:

- Turn the problem into an actionable goal.
- Identify who the key individuals are that need to be consulted and kept informed of progress on the problem.
- Create a succinct, unified sense of purpose and direction for the problem-solving team.

Figure 1.1 Problem statement

1 What problem are we solving? No more than one sentence. The question should have a measurable success target, a deadline for success, and identify the relevant individuals or organisations concerned.

2 Who are the key decision-makers?	**3 What are the criteria for success?**
• Who will decide whether to implement the recommended solutions to the problem? • Is there a senior sponsor within the organisation of this piece of work? • Do you need any advisory help for the work (e.g. steering groups)?	• What are the quality metrics? (e.g. improved or maintained quality) • What are the delivery metrics? (e.g. due by) • What are the people metrics? (e.g. maintained or increased customer satisfaction; improved staff morale) • What are the cost metrics? (e.g. cost impact)

4 What is the context of the work?	**5 What is the scope of the work?**
• Why is the work being done now? • What is the timescale? • What is the historic performance of the organisation? • Has any similar work been carried out in the past?	• What is in scope? • What is out of scope?

6 What are the expected end products?	**7 Who are the problem-solving team members?**
For instance, are you expected to provide a written report, an end presentation, or perhaps a financial model? When are they due by? And who should receive them?	List the team members, their roles, and any significant availability constraints.

How does a problem statement work?

A problem statement should fit on one side of paper and succinctly summarise the key issues that you need to know about the problem you are trying to solve. It poses six questions:

1 What problem are we solving?

This is the most important question in the whole OBTAIN problem-solving process. Your answer here should be no more than a sentence long. It should be time-bound, mention the individuals or organisations concerned, and have a clear, measurable goal that defines 'success' for the workstream or project. For instance, if your company (Peacock Foods) wants to increase its profits by half from a particular foodstuff (crab sticks) within two years, a good 'what problem are we solving?' question would be: 'How can Peacock Foods increase profits from its crab sticks by 150% by 2015 (baseline 2013)?' If you are struggling to summarise the problem in one sentence, ask yourself whether you are dealing with multiple problems (which would each require their own problem statement) or whether you need more guidance regarding what it is you are trying to achieve.

It is important to note that you are making an implicit hypothesis here: that by answering your posed question you are in fact solving your problem. Usually this hypothesis is easy to see. For instance, successfully answering 'how can we increase profits?' would obviously solve a profitability problem. But sometimes things can be more complicated. For instance, you might assume that answering 'how can we bring in more customers to our restaurant?' would solve a profitability problem for the eatery in question, but this may not always be the case (food prices might not cover production costs, for example). In instances like these it is important to sense-check the question you are asking with colleagues, or better still, conduct some analysis to investigate further (see *Chapter 4*).

2 Who are the key decision-makers?

There is a critical distinction to be made here between 'stakeholders' and 'decision-makers' (see *Chapter 7*). An exhaustive list of 'stakeholders' for most problems could probably fill a page on its own; 'key decision-makers' – whilst also being stakeholders – should be only a few individuals. These should include only those individuals who will have an active role in the problem-solving process. For instance, this includes stakeholders who: decide whether to implement your recommendations; are organisation budget-holders; are senior sponsors of the piece of work within your organisation; form steering groups or committees that will act in an advisory role in helping to solve the problem.

3 What are the criteria for success?

These will help you to understand and demonstrate whether you have actually (a) changed anything; and (b) met your desired targets. As such, you should only choose criteria for success which you can actually measure. As shown in Figure 1.1, these criteria should be focused around issues of: quality (i.e. improved or maintained quality measured through percentage defects in production by a given date); delivery (i.e. outputs achieved by a set deadline); people (i.e. staff satisfaction maintained or increased; customer satisfaction increased); and cost (i.e. profits increased by a given percentage by a given deadline). Try to ensure all criteria for success are 'SMART': specific, measurable, achievable, relevant and time-bound.

4 What is the context of the work?

Here the type of questions that should be answered are: why is this a problem now?; what are the key timescales and deadlines?; what are the expected end products (report or presentation)?; and what are the historic issues surrounding the problem? It may be necessary to update this section after you have completed your Value-Context-Performance-Hypotheses (VCPH) pack (see *Section 1.2*).

5 What is the scope of the work?

One of the most frequently encountered issues when trying to solve a problem is 'scope creep'. This is when a problem that once seemed small and manageable gradually gets bigger and bigger in scale. For example, let's say that you work for a biscuits and frozen treats manufacturer. Your boss may have initially asked you to look at increasing sales of lollipops which you agree to, but only after voicing some concerns about your current workload. A little while later she also asks you to take on the issue of increasing ice-cream and biscuit sales, claiming that all along she had in mind that you would look at all three of these products and that you had agreed to this. Clearly the scope of the initial request has changed here. By defining what is agreed to be in and out of scope at the start of a problem and getting your boss to sign off on it, if the scope changes on a request then you can use the problem statement as an audit trail to confirm what was previously agreed.

6 What are the expected end products?

Once you get stuck into OBTAIN problem-solving, it is easy to get carried away with the process and forget that all your good work ultimately requires an end product. It is important to be upfront with whoever has commissioned your work and ask early on what exactly is expected as a final output. This can take many forms: written reports; PowerPoint presentations; spreadsheet models. Whatever is chosen, you should make sure that you are clear what it is and when it is expected by – this way you and your team have a clear and tangible output and deadline to work towards.

7 Who are the problem-solving team members?

Don't forget the most important element – the team. List who they are, what their roles in the team are, and any issues or constraints (i.e. availability) that may be important.

When should you use a problem statement?

A problem statement is the very first tool you should complete when starting the OBTAIN process. Having said this, you may find that in trying to answer some of the questions posed in the problem statement you need further information or even need to conduct some quick analyses. Consequently, you should consider the creation of a problem statement to be a two-step process:

1 Draft the problem statement – answer the questions to the best of your knowledge, flagging up areas where you need clarification on an issue. For instance, you may have been tasked with 'improving retention rates in your organisation', but what does this actually mean and how will your performance in this respect be measured? Thus you need to go back and clarify what it is that you have been asked to do.

2 Revise the problem statement – whilst you may be clear on your objectives and timescales, in following the second stage of the problem-solving process (see *Section 1.2*) you may discover certain unexpected impediments to solving the problem at hand. For instance, if your problem is about retention rates, an unexpected issue might be forthcoming redundancies in certain departments. If this happens, you should revise the problem statement in the light of new information. Try to confine tinkering with the problem statement to the early stages of a problem-solving

process. Think of the problem statement as being like the foundations of a house – once these have been agreed upon and set in the ground you don't want to be changing them when construction begins! Having said this, if as you progress through the OBTAIN process it becomes increasingly obvious that you are solving the wrong problem, stop and return to the start of the problem-solving process. As frustrating as this may be, implementing the wrong solution to the wrong problem will always be worse.

How should you use a problem statement?

A problem statement should be drawn up by the problem-solving team (or individual, if you alone are the problem-solving team) and shared with the key decision-makers for them to agree upon it. This way the team and key decision-makers share a unified vision and approach to the problem. Once the problem statement has been agreed upon, it should be checked regularly in order to avoid the scope and original aims of the work changing or losing focus.

You should ensure that every team member has read and understood the problem statement. If a new member joins the team midway through the problem-solving process, the problem statement and VCPH pack should be the first documents they read to gain familiarity with the problem. See *Chapter 8* for more details on team issues.

Example Let's use a simple example to give us a better idea of what a problem statement looks like in practice. Daniel is Strategy Manager at NewsForce – a national newspaper publisher – which is looking to increase sales of its flagship paper *The Reporter*. Daniel and his team of five have been tasked by the Strategy Director with devising a strategy to increase sales of the publication by 20% by the end of the next financial year. Daniel suggests booking out an hour with his team to go through the first iteration of the problem statement. He takes a piece of blank flip-chart paper and sticks it vertically on the wall. He then writes out the seven boxes and headings of the problem statement (see Figure 1.1) and explains to his team what a problem statement is. He acts as the facilitator as the team jointly discuss each of the questions posed in the problem statement.

Starting with the question 'what problem are we solving?', the team feel the Strategy Director has been quite clear with his request. One of Daniel's team suggested the question be: 'How can we increase sales of *The Reporter*?' Feeling that this was a bit loose, Daniel asked them to think a bit more about who is responsible for the piece of work; how the target will be measured; and when the target needs to be met. The team then agree that Daniel's suggested key question is a lot tighter in its definition: 'How can NewsForce ensure sales of *The Reporter* increase by 20% by the end of 2013/14 from a baseline of 2011/12?'

Regarding the key decision-makers, the team decide that whilst groups like the public, the finance team and the sales team are key stakeholders for the work, they are not key decision-makers. Key decision-makers will ultimately decide whether to implement the recommendations Daniel's team make, whereas stakeholder groups like the sales team will have to act upon the recommendations, regardless of their views on them. As such, the team decide on four key decision-makers: Strategy Director, Chief Executive, Finance Director and a Steering Group for the work. One of Daniel's team suggests that the Steering Group may be a good opportunity to involve other members of the organisation who will be responsible for implementing this strategy, thereby giving them an opportunity to check that the team's suggested recommendations are credible.

For the criteria for success, the team feel that number of sales is the key metric here. However, they are not sure whether profits also need to increase (they may not if the cost of *The Reporter* is reduced), and they assume that the quality of the content of the paper should stay the same. Realising they are not sure about these issues, they create a flag on the problem statement for what they want to check.

All of NewsForce is well aware that newspaper sales generally – and specifically for *The Reporter* – have been declining in recent years. Consequently, this is a key piece of context for the problem statement, but Daniel would like the team to do a bit more research into some figures for this (see *Section 1.2* for how to use a VCPH pack to do this). The team feel that it is important to mention that the Strategy Director is relatively new to the organisation, and thus may want to make a mark on the corporation. Daniel thinks this is an important detail, but conscious that the Strategy Director will be seeing the problem statement, tells the team to keep the point in mind, but that they should not put it in the problem statement for fear of antagonising a key decision-maker.

Regarding scope of the work, the team know that they should only concern themselves with sales of *The Reporter*, but would like to double-check whether there is anything else in or out of scope (see Figure 1.2). For the end products, the team assume that they should deliver both a final presentation to the Strategy Manager and a final report to the key decision-makers (around mid-February, roughly when the Strategy Manager wanted the work finished). Nonetheless, Daniel suggests they should double-check about the end products. Finally, he notes the team members and their staffing commitment to the work.

Daniel shares this first version of the problem statement with the Strategy Director (who he identifies as being the key stakeholder for this work – see *Chapter 7*) whilst his team set to work on the next stage of the problem-solving process – understanding the context of the problem (*Section 1.2*).

In conducting their analysis as part of understanding the context, the team come across a report on the newspaper publishing industry which

Figure 1.2 First problem statement iteration

1 What problem are we solving? How can NewsForce ensure sales of *The Reporter* increase by 20% by the end of 2013/14 from a baseline of 2011/12?	

2 Who are the key decision-makers?
- Chief Executive
- Strategy Director
- Finance Director
- Steering Group (to be confirmed but likely to include members of finance team, strategy team and sales team)

3 What are the criteria for success?
- Increase sales by 20% by 2013/14 (baseline 2011/12)

> Should this include anything about cost of *The Reporter* and quality of content? Check with Strategy Director.

4 What is the context of the work?
- Historic decline in newspaper sales generally and *The Reporter* sales specifically

> Can we be more detailed with figures here?

5 What is the scope of the work?
- In scope – *The Reporter* sales only
- Out of scope – any other NewsForce publications

> Is there anything else out of scope?

6 What are the expected end products?
- End presentations for Strategy Manager (16/3/13)
- Final report for key decision-makers (?)

> Check with Strategy Director.

7 Who are the problem-solving team members?
- Daniel (Lead, full-time)
- Sas (Full-time)
- Hannah (Full-time)
- Zena (Full-time)
- Taryn (Full-time until Oct)
- Sarah (Full-time until Dec)

provides an alarming figure: for the past three years, the national newspaper industry as a whole has declined by 3% each year. Daniel and his team wonder whether a 20% increase in sales is a wildly over-optimistic target, and consequently Daniel agrees to bring this to the attention of the Strategy Director.

Following discussions with the Strategy Director, the targets for the piece of work are revised down to a 10% increase in sales. The team are also informed that the quality of content in *The Reporter* must be maintained, whilst the price of the paper cannot be altered. With regard to end products, the Strategy Director notes that he wants the Steering Group to see an interim update presentation on the work, and that the final report should be delivered to the key decision-makers by mid-March. With this new information, the team finalise their problem statement (Figure 1.3) and are ready to move on to the next part of the problem-solving process – breaking down the issues (see Chapter 2).

Figure 1.3 The team's completed problem statement

1 What problem are we solving?
How can NewsForce ensure sales of *The Reporter* increase by 10% by the end of 2013/14 from a baseline of 2011/12?

2 Who are the key decision-makers?	3 What are the criteria for success?
• Chief Executive • Strategy Director • Finance Director • Steering Group (including members of finance team, strategy team and sales team)	• Increase sales by 10% by 2013/14 (baseline 2011/12) • Maintained quality of content in *The Reporter* (to be tracked as part of NewsForce's annual quality audit)

4 What is the context of the work?	5 What is the scope of the work?
• Year-on-year 3% decline in the UK newspaper publishing industry for the past three years • Sales of *The Reporter* decreased by 0.8% last year (from previous year)	• In scope – *The Reporter* sales only • Out of scope – changes to any other NewsForce publications, and changes in pricing structure of *The Reporter*

6 What are the expected end products?	7 Who are the problem-solving team members?
• Interim presentation for Steering Group (14/2/13) • End presentations for Strategy Manager (16/3/13) • Final report for key decision-makers (23/3/13)	• Daniel (Lead, full-time) • Sas (Full-time) • Hannah (Full-time) • Zena (Full-time) • Taryn (Full-time until Oct) • Sarah (Full-time until Dec)

Tips and tricks

- It may look simple enough, but don't let yourself be rushed into completing the problem statement – this is a crucial part of the problem-solving process.

- Set deadlines for your targets, otherwise the work can drag on indefinitely.

- Make sure you get agreement on the problem statement from your key decision-makers. The start of the problem-solving process is the ideal opportunity to confront any problems of differing visions or expected outcomes from stakeholders head on – leave it too long and it becomes harder to re-forge a common vision.

- Be realistic about what criteria for success you are committing yourself to achieve. It's easy to get carried away with promises about how successful your work can be, but ultimately you will be judged on whether you meet the goals you have set.

- As with all problem-solving tools, stick to the principles they advocate but if necessary tweak the tools to your needs.
- Once the VCPH pack has been completed (*Section 1.2*) check if there are any amendments you wish to make to the 'Context' part of the problem statement.

Summary

- Problem statements are the foundations for a successful problem-solving process as they help you to define the problem at hand.
- They stop you from jumping to a solution, by forcing you to fully define and scope out the problem.
- They are a vital tool for:
  - turning a problem into an achievable goal
  - identifying the key decision-makers involved in solving the problem
  - creating a unified sense of purpose amongst the team.
- Ensure all team members have read and fully understand the problem statement.
- Problem statements can be revised during the early stages of a problem-solving process.
- If you are struggling to express your problem in terms of a problem statement, it is worth considering whether you are actually dealing with multiple problems, or whether you need more information about the problem at hand.

Did you know?

The use of problem statements is not confined to business environments. Often academic research projects – particularly scientific ones – will use a variation of a problem statement to outline their research proposal. This is commonly known as the 'primary research question'.

1.2 The key issues you need to know to solve the problem

Key tool:
- **Value-Context-Performance-Hypotheses (VCPH) pack**

Fundamental principle:
Every problem is a product of its environment – without understanding its environment the problem cannot be solved.

What is a VCPH pack?

Do you ever feel you don't have a good contextual understanding of the work you're doing? Perhaps you feel like you can't see the wood for the trees? Or maybe you know what your work is, but not why it's important to your organisation?

Concerns such as these are all based around a lack of contextual and historic knowledge of an organisation regarding a particular problem. In order to overcome these concerns, you need to understand the context within which the problem has arisen. Creating a *Value-Context-Performance-Hypotheses pack* (VCPH pack) early on in the problem-solving process achieves this by helping you to:

● understand the value to the organisation of the problem you are solving

● contextualise the problem

● compare internal and competitor past performance

● identify the initial hypotheses for solving the problem.

A VCPH pack should contain a series of quick analyses focusing on the history and context around a particular problem. The VCPH framework helps you think through what some of these analyses should be (see Figure 1.4).

Figure 1.4 VCPH framework

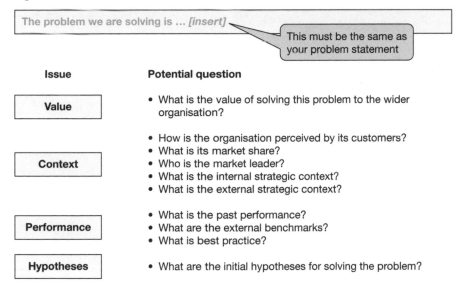

A VCPH pack should answer the questions outlined in Figure 1.4 (note the questions are only suggested and can be changed), and can take the form of either a set of PowerPoint slides or a brief written report.

Each of the four groupings have suggested questions which are vital for understanding the context of a problem, and by answering them you will be in a good position to solve the problem at hand. The importance of knowing these answers can be summarised as follows:

- **Value.** By defining the 'value' (both financial and non-financial) of the problem it becomes easier to explain to reluctant stakeholders why it is important that they help you in solving the problem. For instance, your 'value' analysis might show that by solving your problem of wasted produce you can save your organisation £3m this financial year.

- **Context.** Understanding the context behind a problem can often provide the key insight to solving it. For instance, if your contextual analysis demonstrates that with regard to the external strategic context there is growing concern about redundancies in your sector, this could be a major contributing factor to the problem that you are experiencing – poor productivity in your workforce.

- **Performance.** Most problems are about improving performance. By looking at historic trends (i.e. past performance) you can identify what is actually quite normal compared to what is completely unexpected. Seasonal variation in demand is often a good example of something appearing abnormal over a short period of time, but in fact quite expected when factoring in longer-term trends. External benchmarking can be vital in giving you a sense of whether your problem is unique to your organisation or common to your peers. And best practice analyses can provide key insights when you are devising solutions later, as well as giving a sense of comparison between your organisation and the 'best' (see *Chapter 9* for more on benchmarking).

- **Hypotheses.** Rightly or wrongly, every time you try to solve a problem someone will already have an idea about how to solve it (see *Chapter 3*). Whilst it's absolutely important not to jump to conclusions and circumvent the problem-solving process, at the same time you can't afford to ignore these initial hypotheses. Instead, you should capture them in the VCPH pack, test them in your later analyses (see *Chapter 4*), and if they are wrong, then discard them. The danger in ignoring them is that you risk alienating the people who are forwarding the hypotheses, and you may in fact be missing out on a vital insight.

How does the VCPH pack work?

The VCPH pack should contain a series of quick analyses that relates to the questions in the framework. You may need to ask different members of your organisation to help you with some of these. Table 1.1 shows examples of some of the potential sources.

There are some critical points to remember when completing the VCPH pack:

- You are just laying the foundations for the problem-solving process, not solving the problem yet. You should try to complete the pack as quickly as possible and not get bogged down in detail; if you can't find the answer to one of the questions then move on and come back to it later if necessary.

Table 1.1 Analysis and sources for the VCPH pack

The problem we are solving is ... [insert]			
	Question	Analysis	Potential source
Value	What is the value of this problem to the wider organisation?	Quantitative and qualitative valuation of solving the problem	Information team; finance team; stakeholder discussions
Context	How is the organisation perceived by its customers?	SWOT analysis (see *Chapter 9*)	Team analysis
	What is its market share?	Organisation percentage of total market	Information team
	Who is the market leader?	Market leader in sector	Information team
	What is the internal strategic context?	PESTEL/SWOT analysis (see *Chapter 9*)	Team analysis
	What is the external strategic context?	PESTEL/SWOT analysis (see *Chapter 9*)	Team analysis
Performance	What is the past performance?	Quantitative metrics of past performance	Information team
	What are the external benchmarks?	Quantitative metrics of competitor performance	Industry journals and reports
	What is best practice?	Operational details of best-performing competitors and other industries which deal with similar problems	Industry journals and reports
Hypotheses	What are the initial hypotheses?	List of the initial hypotheses suggested for solving the problem	Team and stakeholder discussions

- Only answer the questions if you think they will be useful to your problem. In some instances, knowing the past performance of the problem at hand might be either very difficult to obtain or not relevant (for instance, there might have been significant operational changes which render past performance analyses unhelpful). If this is the case, don't worry about it and move on.
- Make sure that the pack is intelligible to a lay person. One of the benefits of the VCPH pack is that on a quick read, a new member joining the problem-solving team will be swiftly up to speed on the key issues surrounding the problem. If the language you use in the pack is obtuse and jargonistic, you'll be diminishing the usefulness of the pack.

When should you use the VCPH pack?

Along with the problem statement (see *Section 1.1*), you should regard the VCPH pack as being the foundation of the OBTAIN problem-solving process. Therefore the VCPH pack should be completed shortly after the problem statement. There is some interlinking between the problem statement and the VCPH pack. You should use the outputs of the VCPH pack to fill in any missing details in the 'context' part of the problem statement, or to update the problem statement with any new findings that arise from creating the VCPH pack.

How should you use the VCPH pack?

The VCPH pack is for the benefit of the entire problem-solving team. It should be used as a reference document to remind the team why the problem is important, as well as being a useful input for potential ideas on how to solve the problem (especially through the early identification of hypotheses). Like the problem statement, all team members should be fully acquainted with the contents of the VCPH pack (see *Chapter 8* for more on team issues). By having a single, completed document that the whole team can share, you ensure that everyone is clear about the situation at hand.

Example Edleen works in the corporate development department of a Europe-wide e-learning company called 'E-Z Learn' which provides online courses for adult learners in English, Maths and Sciences. E-Z Learn are contemplating launching a new range of language courses, and the corporate development team have been tasked with investigating the feasibility of this new service line. At a team meeting, Edleen suggests that the team would benefit from under-standing the current state of E-Z Learn before they embark on their research into the new language courses. Her manager agrees and gives Edleen's team some time to complete a preliminary VCPH pack for the issue. After dividing up responsibilities for answering the questions as suggested in Figure 1.5, we can see here what the team came up with.

For answering the questions about 'Value', Edleen asked the Finance Team to help her with some rough estimates, using the problem statement (*Section 1.1*) to help explain to the team what she was working on. The 'Context' section was the output of a long team brainstorming session where Edleen facilitated a SWOT and PESTEL analysis (see *Chapter 9*). The team then selected the most

Figure 1.5 Edleen's VCPH pack for E-Z Learn

> Should E-Z Learn launch a new range of e-learning language courses starting in the financial year 2013/14?

Value

What is the value of solving this problem?
- Based on estimates that the European e-learning language courses market is worth £20m, and that E-Z Learn might get 5% (£1m). Cost of set-up would be £500,000 (of which £250,000 is one-off). *Total potential profit of £0.5m in year 1, rising to £0.75m in year 2 and £1.5m in year 3.*
- Non-financial value in expanding market presence.

Context

How is the company perceived by its customers?
- E-Z Learn's USP is a high quality product (over 85% of customers rate its courses as excellent) at low prices (1/3 price of closest competitor).

What is its market share?
- E-Z Learn holds approximately 10% of the market share.

Who is the market leader?
- LearnLine, the biggest e-learning provider in Europe, with approximately 75% of the market share.

What is the internal strategic context?
- Current turnover £1.8m per annum (£1m profit).
- Concern that company needs to expand its brand presence.
- Has no experience in delivering language courses.
- Most of its clients are repeat customers (60%).

What is the external strategic context?
- Growing demand for qualifications in workforce.
- Improving technology makes online courses easier to use.
- Increasing rates of internet usage across older age profile.
- Possibility that LearnLine will reduce its prices and remove E-Z Learn's USP.
- Potential that at some point in the near future the government will introduce free e-learning language courses; this could result in big contracts.
- Internet host provider costs are expected to rise.

Figure 1.5 Continued

| Performance |

What is the past performance?
- Since entering into the e-learning market three years ago, E-Z Learn has seen a steady rise in profits:

	Year 1	Year 2	Year 3
Turnover (£m)	0.7	0.9	1.5
Profit (£m)	**0.3**	**0.6**	**1**

- Current customer satisfaction rates are high with 85% of customers scoring the products as 'excellent'.

What are the external benchmarks?
- The market leader for e-learning language courses (LearnLine) has 75% of the market share – approximately £15m in income.
- Current customer satisfaction rates for these courses are not known.

What is best practice?
- Learn4U, the second biggest e-learning provider, is believed to have the highest levels of customer satisfaction. Their delivery model is slightly different to E-Z Learn's. Whereas E-Z Learn's courses are all delivered online, Learn4U's courses have a final 'viva' session by telephone. It is believed that Learn4U's cost base is substantially higher than E-Z Learn's.

| Hypotheses |

What are the initial hypotheses for solving the problem?
- Some senior directors feel E-Z Learn should definitely expand into language courses, even if returns are low for a few years – it is the only way to increase brand presence.
- Others believe that the potential rise in internet host costs could provide a key factor in deciding whether to enter the new market or not.

relevant parts of these analyses to fill in the VCPH pack. The 'Performance' information came from the Information Team and some reputable industry journals. The 'Hypotheses' were already common knowledge within the organisation but to make sure, Edleen checked with her boss that her understanding of them was correct.

Having completed the pack, the team felt they had a solid understanding of the context behind the question of whether to expand into e-learning language courses. By knowing the potential value of this decision they fully understood the importance of their work. The contextual and performance knowledge would be useful in pointing them to some early analyses (for example, what would be the financial impact of internet host cost rises?). And by having a clear idea of the initial hypotheses about the decision, the team were well aware that there would be some pressure from within the organisation to come up with an answer that suggested entering the new market would be a wise choice – something that the team must avoid influencing their judgement and analyses.

Tips and tricks

- As soon as the pack is completed, go back to your problem statement (*Section 1.1*) and check if you want to update anything in the 'context' section. Think of the problem statement as the one-page summary that describes the problem, and the VCPH pack as holding much more detailed context about the problem.

- Engage your stakeholders early on by sharing the VCPH pack with them. This will ensure you are transparent in your thinking, and will give stakeholders an opportunity to point out any differences of interpretation.

- Don't confuse the VCPH pack with generating a solution or conducting analysis. The VCPH pack provides information which will be useful when you get around to conducting detailed analysis, but it is not the final analysis itself.

- Don't reinvent the wheel. If decent past performance or benchmarking analysis already exists (either within your organisation or conducted by external bodies) use it if appropriate.

- Don't be afraid to ask for expert advice (look within your organisation first, and if necessary, then outside) when conducting analysis. A lot of time can be saved this way.

- The questions covered in the VCPH pack should be changed as appropriate – they are suggestive only.

Summary

- The VCPH pack provides the foundations for successful problem-solving. It allows you to clarify the key contextual issues surrounding a problem, whilst underscoring why solving the problem is important to your organisation.

- The pack should be completed at the start of the problem-solving process, but it will be useful throughout in:
  - explaining to stakeholders the significance of the problem at hand
  - highlighting the contextual issues that need to be considered when implementing a solution

- providing a baseline for measuring improvements in performance once a solution has been generated
- testing the hypotheses of key stakeholders early on.
- The pack can be used as an early output to share with stakeholders to show your work to date and to check they are happy with your progress.
- Make sure the whole problem-solving team is fully acquainted with the contents and findings of the VCPH pack.

Did you know?

Contextual issues such as regulatory changes can completely reshape industries. For example, the management consulting industry was born from changes to the US regulatory environment. The Glass-Steagall Act of 1933 stopped banks from acting as investment bankers and retail banks for the same companies. Consultants (building on their experience of cost accounting techniques) stepped in to fill the gap. (For more on this see *The World's Newest Profession*, Chris McKenna (2006). Cambridge: Cambridge University Press.)

End of OUTLINE stage checklist

By this point in the OBTAIN problem-solving process you should have:
- a clear definition of the problem at hand
- an understanding of what a good solution will achieve
- clarity on who the key stakeholders are
- clear deadlines and expected outputs from the OBTAIN process
- understanding across the team of the importance of solving the problem
- some initial hypotheses for solving the problem.

Checkpoint: Preliminary presentation to stakeholders

It is highly beneficial to set up a brief presentation for some of your key decision-makers at this point in the OBTAIN process (see *Chapter 7* for more on stakeholder management and communication). Here you can update them on your progress so far and ask for their thoughts on your proposed next steps (see *Section 6.2* for more about creating presentations). Remember that solving the theoretical problem is only half the battle – you need to make sure your key decision-makers are engaged and committed to implement your proposed solution.

Break down the issues

2

Purpose of the BREAKDOWN stage:

To break down the problem at hand into manageable workstreams.

Tools and techniques covered:

- Issue tree
- 2 × 2 prioritisation matrix
- Workplan

Supplementary tools referred to in this chapter are available in *Chapter 9*.

Key outcomes:

- Problem broken down into separate pieces of analysis which, when conducted, will give you the information needed to solve the problem.
- Workplan listing the necessary analyses to solve your problem, prioritised to give you the maximum effort:output ratio for your work.

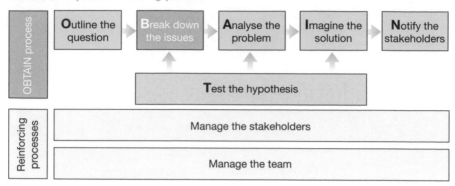

2.1 Untangling the mess

Key tool:
- **Issue tree**

Fundamental principle:

Every problem is made up of constituent parts. If you can identify these constituent parts and address each of them individually you will be able to solve the bigger problem that they form.

What are issue trees?

Have you ever been confronted with a major issue at work but have no idea how to deal with it? Or perhaps you spent weeks deeply engaged in some analytical work, only to realise that it has very little to do with the main problem at hand? Or maybe you worked yourself silly running one particular workstream, only to find that one of your team-mates was already doing exactly the same work as you?

These problems are frighteningly common in the business world, and largely arise due to: a combination of lack of foresight and planning; an inability to look at the problem in its widest sense; and poor team communication. You can overcome and avoid these pitfalls by using *issue trees*.

Issue trees (see Figure 2.1 for a basic template), like all tools and frameworks, are a vehicle for ensuring logical thought and structured planning. However simple this may sound, such logic and structure are often missing in problem-solving. Building from the question 'what problem are we solving?' (i.e. the problem at hand – see *Section 1.1*), issue trees are a vital tool because they:

- break down the problem into manageable chunks
- give you confidence you've looked at the full extent of the problem

Figure 2.1 Issue tree template

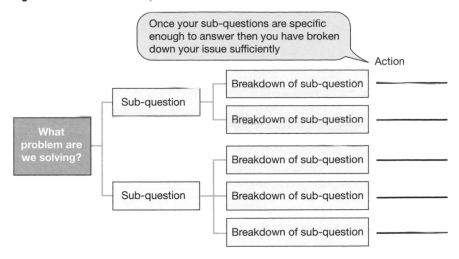

- allow you to delegate responsibility for different analyses which will help solve the problem.

How do issue trees work?

Issue trees are closely linked to *problem statements* and should be used straight after the problem statement is drawn up and the VCPH pack is finished. At the heart of issue trees lies the concept that any problem, no matter how big, is made of constituent parts. If you can correctly identify and address what the constituent parts are, then the problem essentially becomes a series of mini-problems, which is consequently much more manageable to solve.

Issue trees work by setting out the 'problem we are solving' on the left-hand side of the page. Moving from left to right, this question is then broken down into sub-questions which relate to the question preceding them. Eventually, you should get to such a level of disaggregation in your questions on the right-hand side that a discrete piece of analysis can be done to answer the questions at the end of each branch of the tree. By answering these sub-questions you will then be able to answer the original question 'what problem are we solving?'.

There is one key principle you must adhere to when you break down your problem using an issue tree. The principle is that the constituent parts must be 'separate but complete'. In practice this means your issue tree must be:

- Separate – by ensuring that each vertical set of questions can be answered without reference to the other questions in the same vertical set. This is important because if the questions are not separate, then the likelihood is that the actions and analyses that result from the issue tree will be overlapping, and thus duplicate work and effort for whoever conducts the analyses. For instance, if you have two similar sub-questions in an issue tree (such as 'can sales be increased?' and 'are sales too low?') and one person is tasked with answering the former and another the latter, it is likely that there will be overlapping effort from both team members in answering the questions.

- Complete – by ensuring that each vertical set of questions, when taken together, fully answers the preceding question that it relates to. It is vital to ensure that the completeness rule is adhered to – if not, you run the risk of missing an important part of the problem. This is arguably the hardest part of writing an issue tree and as a result it can be helpful to get a friendly eye to look over your issue tree. For instance, if your issue tree is looking at improving productivity, but the sub-questions focus only on output and not input, then the issue tree is not complete as you are missing out an important part of the problem.

When should you use issue trees?

Issue trees should be used straight after the problem statement and VCPH pack have been drawn up. This means that once the scope of a problem is determined, then the issue tree can help to define a sensible course of action as it lays out the analyses needed to solve the problem.

There are two key things that you should remember when using issue trees:

1 Issue trees shouldn't be static – it's very tempting to draw up what seems like a perfect issue tree and stubbornly stick to it even if you receive new information regarding the problem at hand. As frustrating as new information that seems to throw you off course can be, you ignore it at your peril. Just as a stakeholder's demands might change the scope of a problem (though this can be mitigated by the problem statement), so the nature of your analyses and your thinking can change during the problem-solving process too. Issue trees consequently need updating and reiteration.

2 Don't fret if the issue tree isn't perfect – things very rarely are. It's crucial just to get the issue tree *good enough* to take things forward. It can always be 'perfected' later.

Issue trees can be used in all manner of situations. Ultimately their use is in breaking down a problem into manageable parts. This can be applied to any form of problem-solving: from one person hoping to get a quick insight into an issue they are facing to a whole organisation wanting to figure out its strategy for the year ahead.

How should you use issue trees?

Once an issue tree is drawn up, unless it is for the benefit of one person only, it is vital to share the tree with the core team responsible for dealing with the problem at hand. This way everyone knows where the thinking is at on the issue, and the different actions and analyses (on the right-hand side of the tree) can be attributed to different team members.

Example Jonathan is a Vice President of Sales at a major international toy manufacturer. Earlier this morning, Jonathan's boss – the Executive Vice President of Sales – expressed deep concern that profits from the most popular toy the company produces – the 'Bouncy Ball' – have been decreasing over the past few years. Jonathan has been tasked with devising a strategy to turn this product line back to high levels of profitability. The Executive VP is impatient, and wants to know Jonathan's plan of action for looking into the issue by the end of the day. Jonathan has lots of other things on his plate at the moment and knows he will have to delegate much of the responsibility of this work to his sales staff. However, rather than just dump the problem at the door of one of his juniors, Jonathan would prefer to help them on their way by devising an issue tree for them to work from. This way he can be confident that they can get stuck in right away on the analysis, and he will have something positive to tell his boss by the end of the day. Jonathan starts to sketch out an issue tree on some blank paper in front of him.

Jonathan knows that the problem to be solved is around increasing profits from the Bouncy Ball. Consequently, the key question to ask is, 'what do we need to do to increase profits?' At the highest level, profits are determined by two things – increasing revenues and reducing costs – so Jonathan makes these the next vertical tranche of his sub-questions. As you can guess, for revenues, Jonathan now asks the question 'how can we increase revenues?' This is a standard business question, most commonly determined by two factors – prices and volume. In answer to the question 'how to reduce costs?', let's say that raw materials, employee costs, and 'other costs' answer this question (see Figure 2.2). (N.B. it's always helpful to include 'other' in an issue tree because it ensures the principle of 'completeness' is followed – remember this can always be refined later.)

Jonathan is pretty happy with his issue tree as it stands. He's broken down some of the major components of the problem, and now has a list of actions and analyses that he is going to share with his sales team. There's quite a lot he's not 100% sure about – namely what the 'other costs' are – but knows this isn't a major issue as his sales team can now look into this in greater detail. It's only a first draft and will need refining, but with this framework for action provided by the issue tree he feels confident he's in a good position when he chats with his boss later.

A couple of days have passed since Jonathan first drew up his issue tree (Figure 2.2). Since then his team have focused their activities on analysing the costs involved in producing the Bouncy Ball (see *Section 2.2* for more on prioritising work), and have come to the conclusion that there are only minimal opportunities to be gained from reducing costs. Consequently, the focus of the next bit of work will be around how to increase sales. Jonathan's boss was happy with the update he got last time they spoke, but noted that the actions were quite high-level, and said that the next time they meet he wants a greater

THE OBTAIN PROBLEM-SOLVING PROCESS

Figure 2.2 Jonathan's issue tree

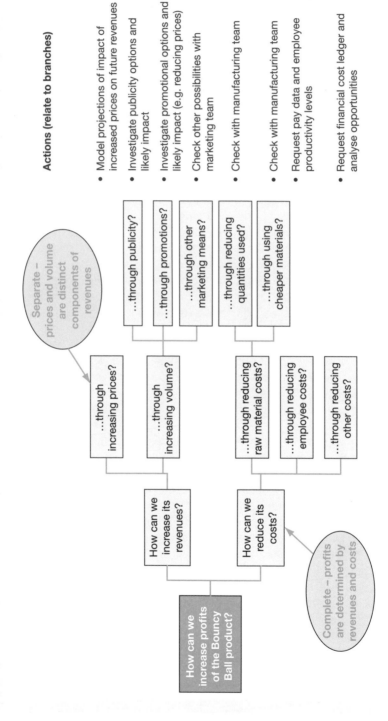

Actions (relate to branches)

• Model projections of impact of increased prices on future revenues

• Investigate publicity options and likely impact

• Investigate promotional options and likely impact (e.g. reducing prices)

• Check other possibilities with marketing team

• Check with manufacturing team

• Check with manufacturing team

• Request pay data and employee productivity levels

• Request financial cost ledger and analyse opportunities

Separate – prices and volume are distinct components of revenues

...through publicity?

...through promotions?

...through other marketing means?

...through reducing quantities used?

...through using cheaper materials?

...through increasing prices?

...through increasing volume?

...through reducing raw material costs?

...through reducing employee costs?

...through reducing other costs?

How can we increase its revenues?

How can we reduce its costs?

How can we increase profits of the Bouncy Ball product?

Complete – profits are determined by revenues and costs

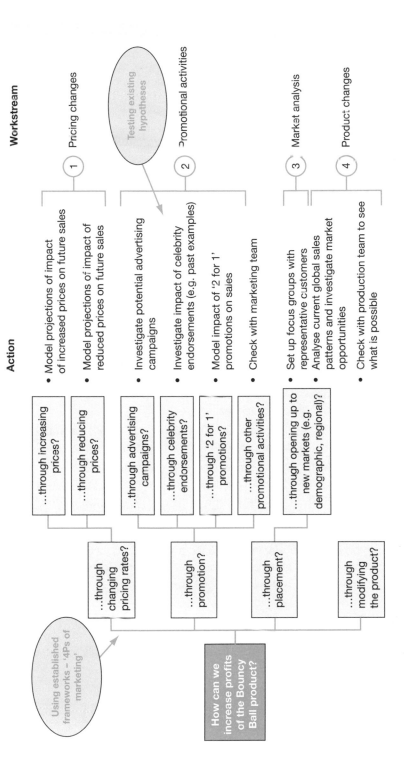

Figure 2.3 The team's revised issue tree

Workstream

(1) Pricing changes

Testing existing hypotheses

(2) Promotional activities

(3) Market analysis

(4) Product changes

Action

- Model projections of impact of increased prices on future sales
- Model projections of impact of reduced prices on future sales

- Investigate potential advertising campaigns
- Investigate impact of celebrity endorsements (e.g. past examples)
- Model impact of '2 for 1' promotions on sales
- Check with marketing team

- Set up focus groups with representative customers
- Analyse current global sales patterns and investigate market opportunities

- Check with production team to see what is possible

...through increasing prices?

...through reducing prices?

...through advertising campaigns?

...through celebrity endorsements?

...through '2 for 1' promotions?

...through other promotional activities?

...through opening up to new markets (e.g. demographic, regional)?

...through changing pricing rates?

...through promotion?

...through placement?

...through modifying the product?

Using established frameworks – '4Ps of marketing'

How can we increase profits of the Bouncy Ball product?

level of specificity in the plan of action. He also thinks that the team should really be considering the effect of celebrity endorsements on sales. Jonathan thinks these were pretty fair comments (though is not so sure of the value of celebrity endorsements), and gathering his team together, suggests they come up with a revised issue tree. Figure 2.3 shows what they came up with.

This time, one of Jonathan's team suggests using a well-known framework as the basis for the issue tree – the 4Ps of marketing ('product, placement, promotion, pricing' – see *Chapter 9*). Breaking down the issue tree into discrete actions on the right-hand side of the tree, Jonathan realises there are four clear workstreams that he can delegate to his team members. Everyone is now clear on the next analyses they need to do, and Jonathan sets them a deadline of two weeks for when he wants to hear the results of their findings. The team leave the meeting confident that the work they will be doing is relevant to the problem at hand, and happy that Jonathan has been transparent in both his thinking and his delegation of the workload.

Tips and tricks

- Don't reinvent the wheel – use established business frameworks to help ensure your tree is 'separate but complete' (see *Chapter 9*). For instance, if the problem is on profit, the first vertical set of sub-questions should probably be about 'revenues' and 'costs'.

- Capture and challenge existing myths and hypotheses in your issue tree, as your stakeholders will be keen to hear about these.

- Always keep focused on the problem you are trying to solve – it is easy to get side-tracked into tangential analyses which aren't crucial in helping you move forward.

- Thinking in numerical terms to establish the 'separate but complete' principle can be helpful. For instance, if your question is around improving productivity per employee, use the equation 'productivity = output quantity / input quantity' and make 'output' (i.e. number of units) and 'input' (number of employees) two sub-questions in your tree.

Summary

- Issue trees are quite simply a tool to help you logically structure your thinking.
- They are useful in:
  - breaking down the problem
  - separating out analyses
  - ensuring the full extent of the problem has been looked at.

- When breaking down a problem, all issue trees should abide by the golden rule of being 'separate but complete'.

- Issue trees should be drawn up after the problem has been scoped out using a 'problem statement', however they should be consistently refined as the work progresses.

- Issue trees don't need to be absolutely perfect – just good enough to help you progress your thinking and enable you to get started with some analysis into the problem.

Did you know?

The principle behind issue trees – breaking down a problem into its constituent parts – is a key concept in the modernisation of the business world. The revolutionary success of the 'assembly line' production method that Henry Ford pioneered in the early twentieth century shares the same key principle of issue trees. By breaking down the production of cars into separate parts that together completed the Model T car, Ford was able to maximise its efficiency.

2.2 Prioritise your workload to maximise your effort: output ratio

Key tools and techniques:
- **2 × 2 prioritisation matrix**
- **Workplan**

Fundamental principle:
Some issues are simply more important than others and should be dealt with accordingly.

What is a 2 × 2 prioritisation matrix?

Do you ever feel that the work you are doing isn't critical to your bigger problems? Maybe you think that your efforts are being wasted by focusing on minor issues? Or perhaps you find it hard to know where to begin when confronted by a long list of tasks?

Worries like these can be solved by prioritising your issues and workload using a 2 × 2 prioritisation matrix. You may have seen variants of a 2 × 2 matrix many times before (two of the most famous of these, the Ansoff Matrix and BCG growth-share matrix, are in *Chapter 9*) and you can use them in all variety of manners. In the problem-solving process, use the matrix to prioritise your workload when you have a series of analyses to conduct which have resulted from your completed issue tree (*Section 2.1*).

How does the 2 × 2 prioritisation matrix work?

A 2 × 2 prioritisation matrix has two axes (as in Figure 2.4). Each of these axes is given a criterion, which then can be divided into 'high' or 'low'. In the OBTAIN problem-solving process, when prioritising actions arising from an issue tree, it is recommended to use definitions such as *'impact of analysis'* and *'need to know pressure'*. In this case, *'impact of analysis'* means how useful you think a piece of analysis will be in helping you solve the problem, and *'need to know pressure'* means how important it is that you receive one piece of analysis sooner than another. Whilst it's important to realise these are very subjective criteria (which you may need to revise in the light of new information), they will nonetheless help you to plot onto the matrix which are the most pressing pieces of analysis.

As shown in Figure 2.4, the analyses and actions arising from your completed issue tree (*Section 2.1*) should be numbered and mapped onto the matrix and scored according to the two criteria on the axes.

Figure 2.4 2 × 2 prioritisation matrix and how the issue tree analyses feed into it

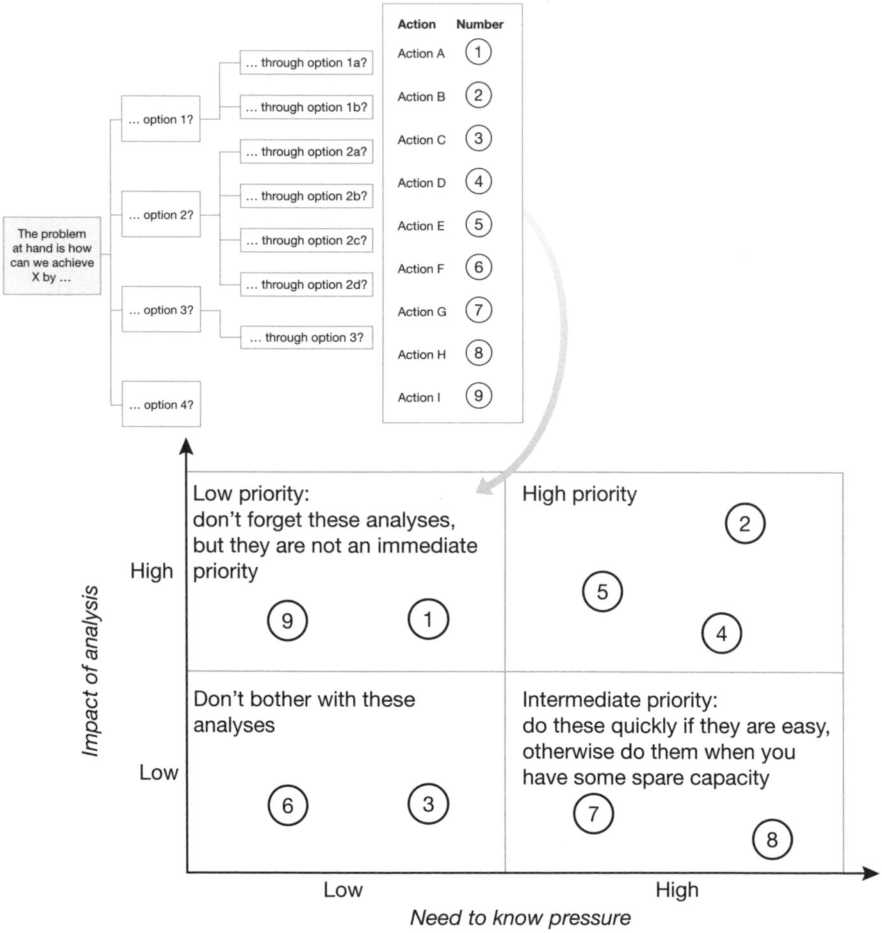

How you score the different analyses by criteria will inevitably be influenced by certain hypotheses you may have about the problem at hand. It's crucial to realise that you may only be thinking about these on a sub-conscious level, and so you must try to bring them out and be explicit about them. For instance, if you are looking to improve employee productivity, your hypothesis might be that productivity is low because morale is low. Therefore in the prioritisation matrix you might judge a 'timesheet/activity analysis' of employees as being less of a priority than 'conducting interviews' with the employees. Whilst your hypothesis may or may not be correct, it is important to recognise that it is still a hypothesis that must be proved or disproved. Once you have done this you can go back to your prioritisation matrix and re-prioritise the analyses based on your refined hypothesis. See *Chapter 3* for more on this.

When should you use the 2 × 2 prioritisation matrix?

The prioritisation matrix should be used after you have finished completing your issue tree (*Section 2.1*). The issue tree should have a series of actions and analyses arising from it, and you should number these and plot them onto the matrix. Once you have identified where the analyses sit in each of the four quadrants you can then assign members of your team to complete them by set dates according to their priority.

How should you use the 2 × 2 prioritisation matrix?

Whilst it's always useful for a group of people to complete business tools together, you can conduct the prioritisation by yourself if you are the team leader. However, you should always make sure to share the completed matrix with your team, along with whoever is responsible for completing each task. This output will be a workplan, like that in Table 2.1.

Once you have your workplan laid out you are ready to move on to the next parts of the OBTAIN problem-solving process: testing the hypothesis (*Chapter 3*) and analysing the problem (*Chapter 4*).

Tips and tricks

- 2 × 2 matrices can be used in all manner of situations – all you need to do is change the criteria on the axes.
- If you want to be more precise when completing the matrix you can quantify your scores across the axes (i.e. 1–5), rather than just 'high' and 'low'.
- Getting other members of your team or key stakeholders to join in the prioritisation is an effective way of ensuring they are engaged in the OBTAIN problem-solving process.

Table 2.1 Workplan arising from prioritisation matrix

Priority	Action/analysis	End product	Responsible	Due	Comment
High	Analysis 2	Spreadsheet model	Gregor	05-Dec	
High	Analysis 5	Data analysis	Gregor	05-Dec	
High	Analysis 4	Interview write-ups	Moazzam	08-Dec	
Intermediate	Analysis 7	Interview write-ups	Ben	15-Dec	
Intermediate	Analysis 8	Brief report	Ben	15-Dec	Only do if spare capacity
Low	Analysis 9	Brief report	Gregor	20-Dec	
Low	Analysis 1	Data analysis	Moazzam	20-Dec	Only do if spare capacity

Example Richard has recently joined the marketing team at a major European football club. The team are currently focusing on increasing merchandise sales in the Far East. His boss has just completed an issue tree and has a list of analyses that he wants Richard to conduct in order to get a better sense of what the merchandise growth strategy options are. Table 2.2 shows the list of analyses filling up Richard's in-tray.

Richard's starting hypothesis (see *Chapter 3* for more on hypotheses) is that it is only sensible to explore increasing merchandise sales in the Far East if the market has not already been saturated by other European football clubs. He consequently prioritises his analyses based on this hypothesis. If he finds that the market is not fully saturated and there could be scope for substantial sales from another football club then he plans to proceed with the further analyses. If the market appears saturated, he intends to go back to his boss and suggest that the team rethink their strategy.

Richard feels it would be sensible first to share with his boss his thoughts about market saturation. Whilst his boss is pretty convinced that there is scope for another major European club to increase merchandise sales in the region, he agrees it would be wise to get some quantitative data on the issue to avoid

Table 2.2 Richard's current in-tray

Action	No.
Market share analysis of sports merchandise in region by European teams	1
Understand manufacturing capacity for extra merchandise	2
Football merchandise revenues broken down by country	3
Analysis of football supporters' average merchandise expenditure in region	4
Model impact of creating region-specific merchandise	5
Impact of advertising on regional television	6
Interviews with regional staff	7
Impact of changing merchandise costs by region	8
Consumer focus group interviews	9
Model impact of football team performance on additional sales	10
Benchmark other football clubs' merchandise sales strategies in region	11
Determine profit margins by merchandise line	12

Table 2.3 Richard's workplan

Ref.	Priority	Action/analysis	End product	Responsible	Due	Comment
1	High	Market share analysis of sports merchandise in region by European teams	Data analysis	Richard	05-Mar	
3	High	Football merchandise revenues broken down by country	Data analysis	Richard	07-Mar	
4	High	Analysis of football supporters' average merchandise expenditure in region	Data analysis	Richard	07-Mar	
12	High	Determine profit margins by merchandise line	Data analysis	Richard	09-Mar	
2	Intermediate	Understand manufacturing capacity for extra merchandise	Spreadsheet model	Richard	TBD	
5	Intermediate	Model impact of creating region-specific merchandise	Spreadsheet model	Richard	TBD	Dependent on outcome of high priority analyses
7	Intermediate	Interviews with regional staff	Interview write-ups	Richard	TBD	
8	Low	Impact of changing merchandise costs by region	Spreadsheet model	Richard	TBD	
9	Low	Consumer focus group interviews	Interview write-ups	Richard	TBD	
11	Low	Benchmark other football clubs' merchandise sales strategies in region	Brief report	Richard	TBD	

any problems further down the line. Richard consequently fills in his prioritisation matrix as in Figure 2.5.

Keen to organise his time and give himself clear deadlines for the work, Richard then draws up a brief workplan which he shares with his boss (see Table 2.3). His boss finds it very helpful that Richard has been transparent and proactive in organising his workload, and is happy that he knows what to expect from Richard and by when.

Figure 2.5 Richard's completed prioritisation matrix

Impact of analysis (vertical axis)

Low priority — High (8, 9)
High priority — (4, 1, 3, 11, 12)
Ignore for the time being — Low (6, 10)
Intermediate priority — (2, 5, 7)

Need to know pressure (horizontal axis: Low — High)

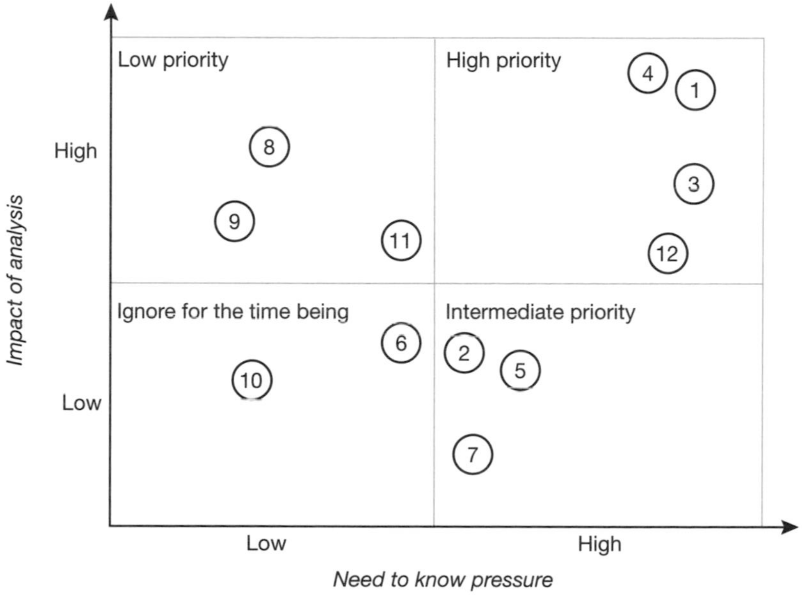

Summary

- Prioritisation matrices help you focus your efforts on the actions which are really important to solving your problem.
- You must always remember that any prioritisation that you make will be the product of your own conscious or subconscious hypotheses about solving a problem. Be explicit about what these are, and if you need to change your hypotheses, be prepared to change your prioritisation matrix too.
- The prioritisation matrix joins the outputs of the issue tree to form a completed workplan. Once you have filled in the workplan you are ready to get stuck into some analysis.

The 2 × 2 matrix owes its origins to the mathematical Cartesian coordinate system developed by the French mathematician and philosopher René Descartes in 1637. However, Descartes is best remembered for his attempts to find indisputable truths which could never be called into question, enshrined in his oft quoted maxim: 'I think, therefore I am.'

End of BREAKDOWN stage checklist

By this point in the OBTAIN problem-solving process you should have:
- broken down your problem into a series of actionable analyses
- prioritised which are the most important issues to be addressed
- drawn up a workplan with deadlines and expected outputs for each of the actions
- assigned each action in your workplan to individuals responsible for their completion.

Test the hypothesis

3

The OBTAIN problem-solving process

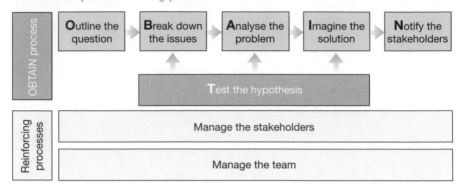

3.1 You are the doctor, the problem is your patient

> **Key tool:**
> ● **Hypothesis tree**
>
> **Fundamental principle:**
> **Problem-solving should be a hypothesis-driven process.**

What is a hypothesis tree?

It may seem counter-intuitive, but when you are problem-solving you should not wait until you have all the facts and then come up with a hypothesis to solve the problem. Rather, you should start with a small number of facts and an initial hypothesis (which could be one of those outlined in the VCPH pack – see *Section 1.2*) early on in the problem-solving process and then test it to see if it is correct – much like a doctor would. If your hypothesis is correct, then you've solved the theoretical problem (though you still need to implement your solution). If not, which is more than likely early on, then you can be sure it's not the right answer and refine the hypothesis or come up with a new one.

You should use a *hypothesis tree* (Figure 3.1) to visually lay out what your hypothesis is and test the logic behind it. In the problem-solving process, this is useful in:

- ● ensuring your hypothesis is logical
- ● identifying what analyses you still need to do to be sure your hypothesis is correct
- ● sharing your thought pattern with the rest of your team.

Figure 3.1 Hypothesis tree blank template

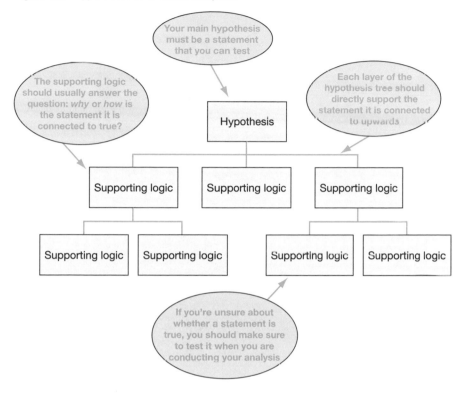

Example Kate's trip to see her parents

A quick example will help show how hypothesising is nothing technical or difficult, and in fact we do it almost all the time. The trick is in being explicit about what your hypothesis is, so that you can check whether it is valid or not.

> *Kate feels like it's about time she flew over to see her parents again who live in New York. Though the cost of the trip is expensive, she has some time off work coming up, and she hasn't seen them for nearly a year. She always enjoys visiting them and feels guilty that it's been so long since she last saw them. She decides that she will book a flight out at the next opportunity.*

Though it may not seem like it, in Kate's mind she has already constructed a hypothesis tree about her decision to fly out and see her parents. Figure 3.2 shows what this might look like written down.

Her hypothesis: 'I am able to fly out to visit my parents in New York' is supported by three pieces of logic:

Figure 3.2 Kate's New York trip hypothesis

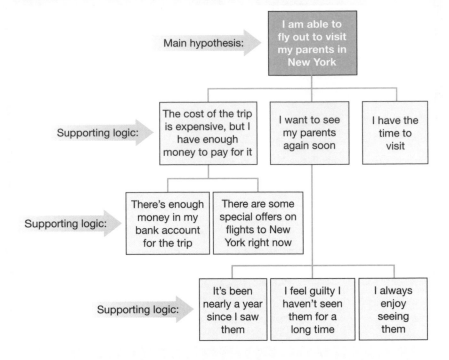

1   The cost of the trip is expensive, but I have enough money to pay for it.

2   I want to see my parents again soon.

3   I have the time to visit.

Two of these three pieces of logic also have further supporting evidence:

1   The cost of the trip is expensive, but I have enough money to pay for it.
 ● There's enough money in my bank account for the trip.
 ● There are some special offers on flights to New York right now.

2   I want to see my parents again soon.
 ● It's been nearly a year since I saw them.
 ● I feel guilty I haven't seen them for a long time.
 ● I always enjoy seeing them.

Kate can now choose to test the logic of her hypothesis by asking: 'Is every one of these supporting pieces of evidence true?' If so, then she has a robust hypothesis and she should book her flights. If one of them is not true (for instance, maybe she no longer has the time to see them) then her hypothesis may be invalid and she may have to rethink her plans.

How does a hypothesis tree work?

Figure 3.3 The hypothesising process

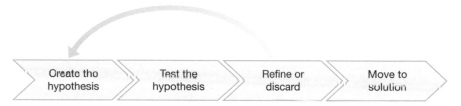

Making a hypothesis is an active process (Figure 3.3). You should start with your initial hypothesis, test it for both its logic and the validity of its supporting statements, and then refine or discard as necessary. Make sure to test your hypothesis with your stakeholders as you progress through the hypothesising process. Your stakeholders can shed invaluable light on your hypothesis, identifying practical constraints to its implementation or adding new information to either support or refute the hypothesis. A good time to test your hypothesis is during an interim report or presentation that updates your stakeholders on your work so far (see _Chapter 6_ for more on writing reports and creating presentations).

As you conduct your analysis (see _Chapter 4_), make sure to add any new information that is relevant to your hypothesis. This will include qualitative and quantitative information that you get from interviews and data analysis, and the identification of root cause issues. Once you're happy that your hypothesis is robust and logical, you can use the insight from your hypothesis to help you devise a solution (_Chapter 5_).

It's very important to recognise that coming up with an invalid hypothesis is a positive contribution to the problem-solving process. Too often we get stuck in the mentality that everything has to be right first time around. This is unrealistic and unhelpful. By testing, refining, and discarding hypotheses you increase and improve your understanding of your problem. In short, sometimes it's good to be wrong!

When should you use hypothesis trees?

The OBTAIN problem-solving process should be _hypothesis-driven_. This means that from early on in the process you should have an idea of what the potential solution to your problem is. The analysis that you conduct in the VCPH pack (_Section 1.2_) as well as that following from your issue tree (_Section 2.1_) will help give you the pieces of evidence to construct your hypothesis tree.

Hypothesis trees can be used in multiple situations and you should feel free to be flexible about how and when you use them. They can be useful in:

- setting a course of action early on
- clarifying and structuring your thinking

- testing initial stakeholder hypotheses and preconceptions
- checking the logic and robustness of your proposed solution
- communicating your thoughts clearly to your stakeholders.

Example Beth has been asked to lead a project to determine whether her company's internet browser product – Highbrowse – should move into the smartphone provider market. The general feeling among the executive team in the company is that the move into the new market is a no-brainer and that the project should be a short one, but Beth is not so sure and so wants to use a hypothesis tree to test the logic and robustness of the decision. At the beginning of the project, based on conversations with the executive team about the rationale for moving into the smartphone market, Beth draws up a hypothesis tree for the current situation (Figure 3.4).

Figure 3.4 Initial Highbrowse hypothesis tree

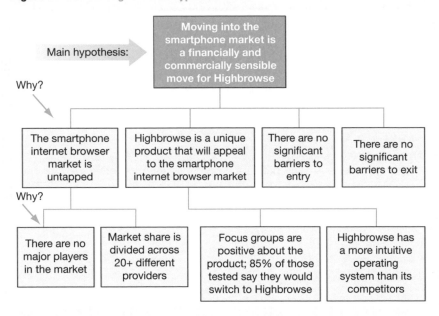

Having laid out the current thinking behind this new market entry strategy (see *Chapter 9* for market entry strategies) in Figure 3.4, Beth wants to check that each of the assumptions is true. Conducting analysis into each of the statements (see *Chapter 4*), Beth finds out that though it is true that the smartphone internet browser market is underdeveloped and that it is likely that Highbrowse will appeal to the target market, her analysis draws into question

Figure 3.5 Beth's annotated hypothesis tree

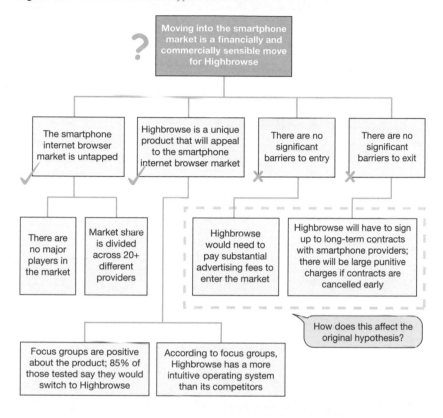

the assumptions that there are no significant barriers to entry and exit. She annotates her hypothesis tree accordingly in Figure 3.5.

These substantial financial barriers to market entry and exit have caused Beth to reappraise the initial hypothesis that the executive team was suggesting (Figure 3.4). As the project lead, she feels she should share with the executive team her thoughts on the issue. Quickly, she draws up a new hypothesis based on her findings as to whether Highbrowse should enter the smartphone market (Figure 3.6).

Using the hypothesis tree structure, Beth decides to write a quick email to the project sponsor on the executive team. She wants to be transparent in her thinking, and give him confidence that she is being proactive in the project. Figure 3.7 is Beth's email.

In sending this email Beth has used hypothesis trees to help her test initial assumptions, refine her own hypotheses, and communicate her thoughts clearly and transparently to her boss.

Figure 3.6 Beth's new hypothesis

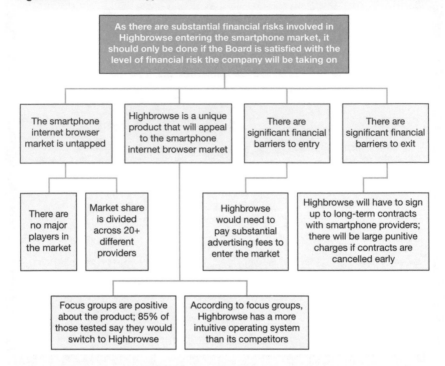

Figure 3.7 Beth's email to her boss regarding Highbrowse

- Don't be afraid to use established tools and frameworks to help kick-start your initial hypothesis. See *Chapter 9* for these.
- To avoid confusing the two, hypothesis trees should run from top to bottom whereas issue trees should run from left to right.
- You don't have to draw hypothesis trees visually – you can just write them in dot-dash (bullet point) format instead.
- Don't worry if you're continuously refining or discarding your hypotheses – testing any hypothesis, no matter how flawed, will help improve your understanding of the problem.

Summary

- Constructing hypotheses is something we do all the time – the trick is in being explicit about what the logic behind our hypotheses is so we can test it.
- The OBTAIN problem-solving process should be hypothesis-driven. This means that you shouldn't be afraid to come up with hypotheses early on, before you have all the information. By testing and refining hypotheses you'll get closer to the eventual solution.
- You can use hypothesis trees in a variety of manners. They are especially useful in:
  - setting a course of action early on
  - clarifying your thinking
  - testing initial stakeholder hypotheses and preconceptions
  - checking the logic and robustness of your proposed solution.

Did you know?

The medical profession is, like the problem-solving process, hypothesis-driven. Working from a series of early observations and information, a doctor will hypothesise what condition his patient has, and if necessary get his team to conduct some tests so he can refine his hypothesis before diagnosing a condition. With so many potential conditions and illnesses, starting with a preliminary hypothesis and then refining it is the best way to treat patients quickly but safely.

End of TEST stage checklist

By this point in the OBTAIN problem-solving process you should have:
- **a clear working hypothesis that you have tested with your stakeholders.**

Remember that testing your hypothesis is something you should do throughout the OBTAIN process. Your hypothesis should be refined, discarded or confirmed as the problem-solving process progresses.

Analyse the problem

4

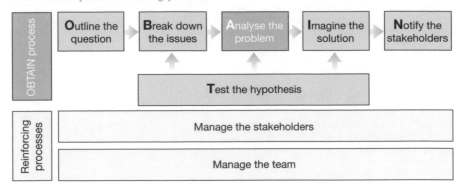

4.1 Without data you have nothing

Key technique:
- **Data gathering**

Fundamental principle:
You cannot solve a problem without data.

Why is data gathering important?

Any successful problem-solving process will be underpinned by robust data and insightful analysis. Far too often in business you see bad decisions being made purely on the back of 'gut feeling', presentations without any charts, reports without any numbers, and solutions without any analysis. In all of these cases, it is likely that little attention was paid to what the data or evidence – the 'cold, hard facts' – actually says. There is a lot to be said about gut instinct, and as we have seen in *Chapter 3*, it can be pivotal in getting the ball rolling with some early ideas about the problem at hand. But on its own it is never enough, and it always needs to be complemented with robust data analysis (see Table 4.1). To make this happen, you need to start with good *data gathering*.

What is data?

Many people have the impression that data is just about numbers, and therefore a job for the IT or information team but not for themselves. This is wrong. Data is any form of information that will help you in your analysis. Data can take two forms: qualitative or quantitative (see Table 4.1 for the different types of data that exist). As such, *data gathering* is the process whereby this information is collected so that the analysis can begin.

Table 4.1 Types of data

Type of data	Examples	Form of analysis appeals to...	Can be used in...	Problems with data include...
Quantitative	Surveys, financials, inventory lists, etc.	Logical side of understanding	Producing tables and charts	Not enough context
			Statistical analysis	Gives false impression of accuracy
			Robust, logical arguments	Too 'cold'
Qualitative	Interviews, case studies, literature reviews, etc.	Empathetic side of reasoning	Providing contextual understanding	Lacking in reliability
			Explaining the human side	Insufficient without quantitative data
			Giving depth and flavour	Too 'soft'

What is the data gathering process?

Data gathering is a six-step process. It follows on immediately from when the workplan for the problem-solving process has been drawn up (*Section 2.2*). Therefore as in Table 2.3 earlier, you will have a list of analyses that need to be conducted, and each one of these will need you to go through the process below.

1 Understand what you want

Unless you have a clear idea of what data you want, your request is doomed to fail. Your workplan (*Section 2.2*) will give you a clear idea of the analysis you wish to conduct. From this, the sort of data you need should be clear. So if your analysis is looking for 'shop-floor employees' thoughts on the new operating machinery' then you probably want some qualitative data on this via interviews with some employee groups. Conversely, if you wanted information on the running costs of the new operating machinery, you might need some quantitative data from the finance team broken down by capital and operating expenditure.

Once you know what data you want, you need to find out where to get it from. Often, however, there may be different sources providing slightly different kinds of data. In this instance, you should consider things like ease of access against the quality of the data needed (a 2 × 2 matrix – see *Section 2.2* for how to construct one – might be useful here).

For example, let's say you want to understand the global market leaders in the provision of cookie cutters. Your company might have done some work on this 10 years ago, producing some charts and tables in a slide-pack which you can easily access, but the raw data (i.e. in a readily analysable form like a spreadsheet) is missing. There is also a private company that provides up-to-date international raw data on the cookie cutter market, but this data is expensive to obtain and will take several weeks to be delivered. Which form of data is better for your needs here? The easily accessible one (your company's old research) which is out-of-date and not easily analysable, or the expensive but up-to-date one (private market research company) which will take some time to arrive? To answer this you need to weigh up the different issues: how important is it that the data is up-to-date; how much time do you have; is there a tight budget for the work; do you want to do some complex analysis on the data?

Once you have decided on the data source you then need to find the contact details for the data holder. In the above example, the contact for your company's old research might be a colleague who worked on the research, whereas the private company contact might be an email address on their website or a telephone number.

Sometimes data will be freely available – from libraries, trade journals or, of course, the internet. In the case of the internet, there is a wealth of free data that can be found with a few clicks of a button; from World Health Organisation statistics on country produce to OECD data on global economic trends to senior executive interviews in the *Harvard Business Review*. If you do choose to use this data, make sure to always cite the source of it in your analysis. For these and other freely available data, it isn't necessary to follow the next parts of the data gathering process (points 3 to 6).

3 Be specific with your data requests and give context

Ask any information team or finance team member what one of their biggest gripes is. They'll undoubtedly mention data requests which people make that are completely vague and utterly unhelpful. The key to a successful data request is to make the request as easy as possible for the data holder to complete. So if you want to know the expenditure on stationery of a particular business unit in your organisation, don't call up someone in the finance team and say something like: 'I need the financials for the past few years for business unit 1 soon.' Instead, be specific and say: 'I'm looking at stationery costs in the business units. Can I have the expenditure split by line item for business unit 1 for the last three full financial years in a spreadsheet by next Monday please?' Or if you're unsure of what you're looking for, give the context and ask for help: 'I'm hoping to analyse stationery costs for the different business units for the past few years. Could you possibly let me know what sort of data you might have on this?' It's good to ask for help. It's bad to waste people's time with vague requests.

4 Incentivise the data supplier

Asking for data often involves asking for a favour. You may not have met the data supplier before, they may have lots of other people asking for data, or you may be looking to negotiate down the supplier on price or expected delivery date of the data. There are no easy rules for negotiation in these situations, but below are some ideas that you might want to try if you're having trouble getting that critical data:

- **Make human contact.** Go and see the data supplier if they work in your building, or call them by telephone if they are external. Someone is much more likely to respond to you quickly if they see you as a real person with stresses and deadlines like them, rather than someone who is just a few words in an email.

- **Offer something in return.** If you're looking to interview someone for some qualitative data, offer to buy them a coffee and conduct the interview then. Or if you're hoping to haggle down an external market research provider on price or deadline, let them know that if they do a good job on this work then you'll be likely to use them again in the future or recommend them to a colleague.

- **State the importance of the situation.** If you're desperate to get the data as soon as possible, then let the data holder know why if it's likely to incentivise them (unless for reasons of confidentiality it would be inappropriate to do so). For example, if the data is needed for a critical report deadline the next day, the supplier is more likely to empathise with your situation than if all they know is that you need the data 'now!'.

- **Appeal to their values and interests.** Try to put yourself in the position of the data holder. What would make them want to get you the data as soon as possible? Perhaps they are frustrated by inefficiencies in your organisation and you are working on ways to improve this, and hence are making the data request. In this case, let them know what the work is about and explain that in helping you they are also helping to reduce inefficiency in the organisation.

- **Make the data request as easy as possible.** Make the data request easy for the supplier. It goes without saying that they are less likely to complete it quickly if it's complicated and needs clarification than if it's straightforward and clear.

5 Make sure the data is correct

The first thing you should do on receiving the data request is to check that everything is in order. Make sure that it corresponds with what you requested; check that the numbers seem sensible; maybe even ask a colleague to look over the data too. It's important that you do this not only because you should always check that data is robust, but because the time immediately after receiving your data is the best time to contact the data supplier with any queries. Leave it too late and they are likely to have forgotten your request or moved on to another priority. If you do spot an error, contact the supplier immediately and politely explain the situation. Once they have committed to providing you with the data in the first place, it's reasonable to expect that the data you receive is correct.

6 Say thank you
Simple, obvious, and horrifyingly uncommon. Not only is it just plain good manners to thank someone, you may need their help in future and want to stay on good terms.

Example Alf works as Assistant Medical Director for a medium-sized private hospital. The hospital has been struggling with throughput, with some patients staying longer than expected in the hospital. Alf wants to know what the profile of these patients is (for instance, by age, condition, gender, etc.), and consequently how to deal with it. To do this, he will need to gather some data before conducting his analysis.

Table 4.2 Alf's workplan

Priority	Action/ analysis	End product	Responsible	Due
High	Length of stay by patient group	Report on patient profiles who are staying the longest in hospital	Alf	15-Dec

Alf starts by looking at his workplan (Table 4.2). Thinking about the first stage of the data gathering process – Understand what you want – he decides that whilst he wants his analysis to be largely quantitative, he also wants to include some qualitative commentary. Thus he decides that for his quantitative analysis, he will look at the last two full years of hospital activity and look at every single admitted patient with information on the patient's age, sex, condition they were admitted for, and any long-term conditions they may have. He knows that the hospital already keeps all of this information so it should be relatively quick to acquire. For the qualitative data, he wants to hear the nurses' perspective on why patients are staying for a long time in hospital and so he decides to set up some interviews with various nurses from the different hospital wards. As a result Alf identifies the sources for the data as shown in Table 4.3.

In making his data requests, for the quantitative request Alf goes to the information team to discuss with Camilla – an information team member who he has received data from before – the data he needs. For the qualitative

Table 4.3 Alf's data sources

Priority	Action/ analysis	Analysis type	Data required	Data source
High	Length of stay by patient group	Quantitative	Hospital activity data for the last two full years for every admitted patient, with details of patient's age, sex, reason for admission, and any long-term illnesses they have	Hospital information team (Camilla M)
		Qualitative	Interviews with ward nurses about long-staying patients	Ward A (Genevieve C)
			Interviews with ward nurses about long-staying patients	Ward B (Caroline S)
			Interviews with ward nurses about long-staying patients	Ward C (Joe L)

interviews, Alf calls each of the senior nurses on the wards to set up some time with either them or one of the junior nurses to discuss the long-staying patients. One of the nurses is worried that the interviews will take time away from more important work – dealing with patients. Appealing to the nurse's values of always putting the patients first, Alf explains that in participating in the interview the nurse is helping Alf improve patient safety and experience by reducing long hospital stays: the aim of his work. Through understanding this context the nurse is a lot happier to give up her time for the interview.

On receiving the data from Camilla, Alf checks it through by comparing it with data which he already has for previous years. He looks for any unexpected trends or unexplained differences compared with the data from previous years. Not finding any, he calls Camilla to thank her for her help. With the nurses (see *Section 4.2* for how to conduct interviews) Alf sends them back a write-up of the interviews for them to check and thanks them for their time and help. Receiving only minor edits from the nurses, he is now ready to crack on with some analysis.

- It helps to involve as many team members as possible when thinking about data sources – the more people involved, the more data sources you are likely to come up with.
- Never confine yourself to purely quantitative data – you need the context and humanising element that qualitative data brings to generate really insightful analysis.
- When making data requests, it can be helpful to send examples of similar data requests that you've made before, or even to draw up a table of the different column headings that you hope to receive the data in.
- Always state what format you want to receive quantitative data in. Avoid at all costs people sending you reams of printed paper – this is very hard to analyse.
- Give an explicit deadline for when you need the data by – people are much more likely to remember this way.

Summary

- Gathering data is vital in allowing you to conduct insightful analysis. Without it no problem-solving process will succeed.
- You should think about your data sources early on in the problem-solving process – ideally immediately after you have drawn your workplan.
- Don't confine your data merely to numbers – interviews are very useful data sources too.
- When choosing your data you may need to weight considerations such as time, cost, level of detail, etc.
- There are six steps to a successful data gathering process:
  1. Understand what you want.
  2. Source the data.
  3. Be specific with your data requests and give context.
  4. Incentivise the data supplier.
  5. Make sure the data is correct.
  6. Say thank you!

Did you know?

The word *data* comes from the Latin term *datum* which means 'that which is given'. The first known use of the term data as a collection of information came from the unlikely pen of the theologian Henry Hammond. In the mid-seventeenth century he wrote: 'From all this heap of data it would not follow that it was necessary.'

4.2 Insightful interviewing

> **Key technique:**
> ● **Interviewing**
>
> **Fundamental principle:**
> Interviewing is a method of qualitative analysis that requires careful planning and preparation like any other form of analysis.

What is interviewing?

Have you ever had an interview where nothing was really discussed? Or perhaps you sat through an interview where there seemed to be no structure to the proceedings? Or maybe you conducted what you felt was a really useful interview, only to forget most of it by the time you came round to writing it up? All of these points are down to bad interviewing technique. Happily this can be easily corrected with good planning.

At its core, interviewing is about extracting information from one person (or a group of people). Whether you are asking for someone's thoughts on your current hypothesis, interviewing someone for a job, or even looking for a flatmate, you are looking to get some information out of the interview that you didn't know before.

Clearly, then, interviewing is about achieving a goal (obtaining certain information from someone), and so just like any goal, to successfully meet it you must know what your goal is and plan how to get it. This will all sound very simple, but if you recognise any of the issues mentioned above from your own experiences, you'll know how often these simple rules are ignored.

How does successful interviewing work?

Successful interviewing is about getting right the three different stages of the interviewing process: pre, during and post. Figure 4.1 lays out what you need to do in each stage.

The *pre* stage is all about preparation. Before you even think of setting up an interview, ask yourself what do you hope to get out of this interview, and who is the right person to interview? It is absolutely crucial that you prepare an agenda for the interview and questions to ask. An issue tree (*Section 2.1*) can be useful in helping you structure an agenda, grouping you questions into sensible sections. It cannot be stressed enough that failure to prepare for an interview (or any meeting, for that matter) is an absolute guarantee of a poor interview. It is always polite and good practice to send the interviewee a draft agenda before an interview and explain why the interview is taking place. Not only does this prepare them for what to expect (especially if they are nervous about the interview), it might give them time to research some of the questions that you are planning on asking.

Figure 4.1 The interview planning stages

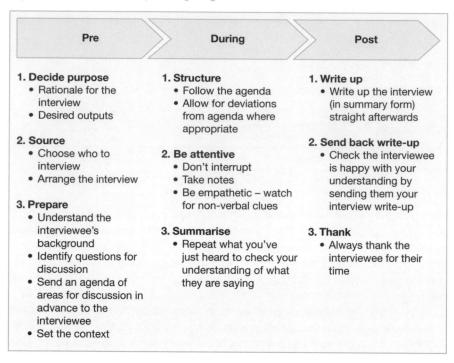

Pre	During	Post
1. Decide purpose • Rationale for the interview • Desired outputs	**1. Structure** • Follow the agenda • Allow for deviations from agenda where appropriate	**1. Write up** • Write up the interview (in summary form) straight afterwards
2. Source • Choose who to interview • Arrange the interview	**2. Be attentive** • Don't interrupt • Take notes • Be empathetic – watch for non-verbal clues	**2. Send back write-up** • Check the interviewee is happy with your understanding by sending them your interview write-up
3. Prepare • Understand the interviewee's background • Identify questions for discussion • Send an agenda of areas for discussion in advance to the interviewee • Set the context	**3. Summarise** • Repeat what you've just heard to check your understanding of what they are saying	**3. Thank** • Always thank the interviewee for their time

Whilst the *during* stage points are the most obvious, they should not be forgotten. An agenda provides invaluable structure to an interview, and makes it easier to write up notes afterwards as it should be easy to trace what part of the agenda your notes relate to. Similarly, though you may often feel you are 'being attentive', check yourself. Are you interrupting the interviewee or finishing their sentences? Are you making eye contact with them or looking at the floor? Even if you are recording the conversation, it is worth taking notes – it makes you look like you are listening and following the interviewee. Watch for body language too. Many behavioural research studies have shown that a person mirroring your body language (for instance, both of you have your legs crossed and are leaning forward in your chairs) is at ease with you. Similarly, if someone is leaning back with their arms folded and averting eye contact, it's pretty likely they don't feel comfortable. Offer them a coffee or glass of water to show a more human side. Finally, make sure you summarise what the interviewee is saying during the interview. Not only does this show you are listening, it helps the interviewee get a sense of what they are saying (which isn't always obvious if you feel pressurised or nervous when being interviewed) and how you are interpreting it.

The *post* stage is just as important as the two which precede it, because this is where you secure the outputs of your interview. Firstly, though it is amazingly tempting to leave the write-up of your interview till later, avoid this at all costs. We all know the scenario: other work gets in the way; maybe the work day is over; or something urgent crops up. Regardless, if you do not write up the interview within at most 12 hours of conducting it, you will without doubt forget some elements of it. No matter how good your notes are, or whether you recorded the conversation or not, you should write up the interview as soon as possible. Make sure to include (for your own purposes only) any non-verbal issues you noted, such as the interviewee seemed agitated or distracted or eager to please. They could be useful pieces of information later. Secondly, just as it is good practice to send an interview agenda in advance, so it is to send a write-up to the interviewee afterwards. This way you can clarify any issues that you missed or misunderstanding that arose, and it gives the interviewee a chance to check their own thinking. And finally, always thank the interviewee for their time.

When should you use interviewing?

Interviewing is crucial in all stages of the OBTAIN problem-solving process, whether you are:

- getting stakeholder thoughts and initial hypotheses at the start of the process
- interviewing potential team members to join the process
- gathering data to inform your analysis
- testing your analysis and hypothesis with stakeholders.

The outputs from your interview should always feed into your hypothesis (*Section 3.1*) about the problem at hand. Remember that only by building up a robust hypothesis that incorporates the insights you have gathered from your quantitative and qualitative analysis will you reach an optimal solution to your problem.

Who should conduct interviews?

In theory any team member should be able to conduct an interview provided they have a decent understanding of the topic being discussed and follow the interview planning stages (see Figure 4.1). This is because any confusion regarding the questions being asked should be cleared up before the interview takes place (in the *pre* stage when the interviewee is sent the questions or agenda in advance), and a good interview structure should be easy for any team member to follow.

In practice, however, there may be some instances where it is inappropriate for some team members to conduct interviews. For example, a senior interviewee in an organisation may feel uncomfortable being interviewed by a junior team member, or a subject expert might feel frustrated being interviewed by a complete novice in a subject area. In these instances, it is important to consider the levels of trust (see *Section 7.2*) that a potential interviewer has before assigning responsibility for interviews.

As with all analyses, the outputs from interviews should be shared with the problem-solving team. Similarly, a team session might be appropriate to draw up an issue tree (*Section 2.1*) to help create a good interview structure.

Example Gabriel is the Organisational Development Manager for a small chain of book and stationery shops – Books & Else – that operates in the United Kingdom. He's concerned by the very poor recent staff satisfaction results from the company annual survey (Table 4.4).

Table 4.4 Staff survey results

Books & Else: Annual staff survey					
Position	No. of staff	Question	Very	Somewhat	Not at all
Shop attendant	36	How satisfied are you in your job?	3%	57%	40%

Gabriel wants to understand the root causes behind these poor staff satisfaction scores so he can recommend a strategy to the board to improve them. He decides that the best way to get to the bottom of this is by setting up a series of interviews with staff from each of the nine shops across the country, some of which he will conduct by phone, others he will travel to.

Thinking about the interview planning stages (Figure 4.1) he starts to plan his questionnaire.

Gabriel identifies the key issues in the *pre* stage as follows:

1 Purpose

- Aim is to understand why staff satisfaction rates are so low.
- Desired outputs are a series of interviews with the shop attendant staff with write-ups which help identify common themes or reasons for staff dissatisfaction.

2 Source

- The shop attendant staff at Books & Else are the sources for the interviews.
- There is not enough time to interview all staff, so Gabriel will interview half (18 staff) on the assumption that this is representative. He will interview an equal number of staff from all nine shops – two from each shop. These will be decided at random.
- Gabriel needs to contact each Shop Manager to ask them to set up staff interviews. Those within a 50-mile radius of London Gabriel will travel to in person, the rest of the interviews will be conducted by telephone.

3 Prepare

- Gabriel's ongoing hypothesis is that staff are unhappy because many of them are on short-term contracts and poorly remunerated. However, he is not blind to the possibility that other reasons exist, and so he constructs an interview guide that he feels covers all possible issues.

- Rather than reinvent the wheel, Gabriel chooses a well-known framework for organisational success – McKinsey's 7S framework (see *Chapter 9*) – to structure the interview. Figure 4.2 shows what he came up with.

Finally, Gabriel sends the interviewees an email with the suggested interview guide (Figure 4.2) as well as a brief note explaining why the interviews are taking place. Here he describes how he is looking to improve staff satisfaction,

Figure 4.2 Gabriel's interview guide

Books & Else Staff Satisfaction Investigation – Interview Guide

Staff role: _____ Staff age: _____ Staff gender: _____ Staff contract type: _____

Questions:
1. Why do you think staff satisfaction is low at Books & Else?

Shared values
2. What do you think are the core values of Books & Else?

Strategy
3. What do you think of the five-year strategy for Books & Else?
4. Where do you see yourself as part of this strategy?

Structure
5. How close do you feel to other parts of the organisation?
6. Do you think your shop operates in an efficient way?

System
7. Do you feel it is possible for you to advance career-wise at Books & Else?
8. Do you think your financial remuneration is a fair reflection of your contribution?

Staff
9. Do you get on well with your fellow employees?
10. How many staff are there usually in the shop on a day-to-day basis?

Style
11. Do you have a good relationship with the shop manager?
12. How would you characterise the management style?

Skill
13. Do you think your skills are well utilised?

Do you have any other thoughts on staff satisfaction?
Do you have any questions for me?

---

and explains that all responses are confidential and will not be used in any way against the staff in future. He receives no amendments back from his email, so he moves on to the next stage of the interviewing process.

- **During the interviews**, Gabriel makes sure to put the staff at ease at all times – stressing that all answers are non-judgemental, confidential and are aimed at improving staff satisfaction. He is careful not to veer from the interview guide too much, though if he feels the interviewee has something interesting to say about something not covered in the guide (for example at one point, an interviewee talks about their experiences at other bookshops) he is keen to hear it.
- **Post interviews** Gabriel makes sure to write up his findings immediately and share them with the interviewees for comments. Once he has completed his 18 interviews, he begins to tease out some common themes – the root causes of the problem – which help him build a new hypothesis (*Chapter 3*) for low staff satisfaction at Books & Else. In doing so, he is surprised to find that the evidence suggests that his ingoing hypothesis was wrong: short-term contracts and relatively low pay do not seem to be driving low staff morale. Instead, a commonly held belief that there is no possibility of career progression or development at Books & Else seems to be the major factor in the poor satisfaction scores.

Tips and tricks

- Always be honest in interviews – it will be obvious to the interviewee if you're not.
- If you can, take a note taker to the interview. This will allow you to dedicate yourself to the interview, rather than worrying about simultaneous note taking.
- Ask a combination of open ('what do you think about…?') and closed ('how many emails do you send a day?') questions to get a balance and rhythm to the interview.
- Check your body language during the interview – if you're leaning in you might appear aggressive or if you have your arms folded you might appear defensive.
- Check out the location for your interview beforehand where possible. Things like room temperature, sunlight, chairs, desk height, etc. can all affect the mood of an interview.
- Be flexible in the interview. Your interview guide may have missed out an area which the interviewee wants to talk about and is relevant to the problem at hand – let them talk even if it means diverting from the guide slightly.

Summary

- Interviews are a form of analysis (qualitative) and should be treated with the same care and planning as any other analysis.
- Interviews can be used at various points in the problem-solving process: setting up the team; testing hypotheses with stakeholders; or gathering data.
- Good interview planning requires effort in three distinct stages: pre; during; and post-interview. Each is equally important.
- Think about who you want to conduct your interviews and how the interviewees might react to them.

Did you know?

Qualitative data and the research it entails is a key part of modern business methods. The growing emphasis on customer satisfaction in the past 40 years has been intertwined with increasing numbers of customer satisfaction surveys and consumer product testing – obvious examples of qualitative research.

4.3 If you want to get to the root cause of the problem, just ask 'why?'

> **Key tool:**
> - **5 whys**
>
> **Fundamental principle:**
> **Getting to the root cause of a problem is crucial in effective problem-solving.**

What is the 5 whys tool?

Let's imagine that one of your more junior colleagues was meant to provide you with some work on a project you are both working on. You ask in the morning where the work is, only to be told rather sheepishly by them: 'I'm really sorry, I just didn't have time.' As a result, you now have to do the work yourself, a crucial deadline may get missed, and you are deeply annoyed with your colleague. On the face of it, your colleague messed up because they couldn't manage their time and that's the lesson you learn from this incident – your colleague is bad at time management.

But this isn't the whole story. Had you probed a little deeper and asked your colleague 'why didn't you have the time to do the work?' they would have said it was because they had other pressing deadlines to attend to. Had you gone further and asked 'why' your colleague prioritised these over your work, you would have discovered that it was because yesterday morning you gave this same colleague a whole heap of other work to do for today and told them it was 'top priority'. Having forgotten about this request yourself, you now realise that whilst your colleague was culpable of not communicating their workload problems to you, the root cause of the problem is you overloading your colleague with work. You would have uncovered this by asking: why?, why?, why? In a nutshell, this is the 5 *whys* tool.

The 5 whys process is useful for two reasons:

1 It gets to the root cause of a problem, rather than just the superficial issues.

2 It is devastatingly simple to use.

However, you should use the 5 whys with caution. Firstly, because of its simplicity, it may not be sophisticated enough for more complex questions – though there is no harm in trying. Secondly, because of the inherent nature of questioning, it can be very easy to be totally subjective when answering the whys. This is a dangerous trap to fall into, so where possible always try to back up your answers with further analysis.

How does the 5 whys tool work?

1 Start with a statement you wish to understand.

2 Ask why this statement is true.

3 For the reason given why the statement is true, ask why again.

4 Keep asking why until you cannot answer why any more.

5 You now have identified the root cause of your problem.

Note: 5 whys is just the name of the tool – don't feel constrained by the number five. Some root causes can be ascertained by less than five 'whys'; others may need more.

Example Francis, the Store Manager at a convenience shop, is trying to understand why past-sell-by-date milk was sold to customers the previous

Figure 4.3 Convenience store 5 whys

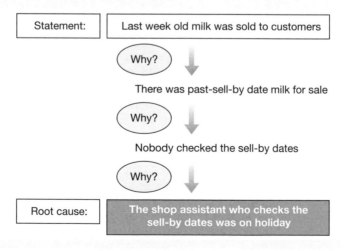

week. She decides to conduct a quick 5 whys on some flip chart paper with the store employees. Figure 4.3 shows what they came up with.

Uncovering that the root cause of the problem was that the shop assistant whose role it is to check the sell-by dates was on holiday, Francis then uses this information to generate a solution to her problem (see *Chapter 5* for how to generate solutions). In this instance, she proposes a new system whereby the duties of anyone on holiday or sick leave are shared between the rest of the staff. Her quick 5 whys helped her get to the bottom of the problem and come up with a simple yet effective solution.

When should you use the 5 whys tool?

The 5 whys tool can be useful at any stage in the OBTAIN problem-solving process: from choosing your criteria for success to devising an implementation strategy. At its core, though, it is an analytical tool and so you are most likely to use it during the analysis phase of the process.

Once you have uncovered the root causes of your problem you must make sure to use this information in both your hypothesis tree (*Chapter 3*) and when you are generating the solution to your problem (*Chapter 5*).

How should you use the 5 whys tool?

Anyone can use the 5 whys tool. However, if you are looking to get to the bottom of a problem which you weren't directly involved in then it is always best to get the input of those who were involved. Your assumptions about an incident or problem will never be a match for the insight of those who experienced it first-hand.

Tips and tricks

- Use a flip chart when conducting the 5 whys analysis in group – this makes it easier for everyone to see.

- Don't be put off by the simplicity of the 5 whys. This is a tried and trusted tool used by many manufacturing companies throughout the world.

- Sometimes 5 whys can break off into different branches – in other words there may be multiple causes for why a statement is true. Complete the 5 whys for each branch until you find the root cause for each. You should find one root cause shared across the branches – this is the main root cause of your problem.

- Always try to back up your root cause findings with either quantitative or qualitative analysis – this will give them more credibility.

Summary

- 5 whys is a delightfully simple tool which allows you to get to the root cause of a problem.
- Always try to engage the thoughts and insights of the people directly involved in the problem.
- 5 whys analysis is inherently subjective by nature, so try to back it up with further qualitative and quantitative analysis.
- Once you have discovered the root cause of your problem, make sure to feed this into your solutions generation.

Did you know?

The 5 whys was made popular by the Toyota Production System in the 1970s. It was invented by the famous Japanese inventor Sakichi Toyoda – founder of Toyota Industries Co. Ltd in 1926. After the post-Second World War 'Japanese economic miracle', Western companies increasingly sought to emulate Japanese business techniques in the 1980s and 1990s.

4.4 Making spreadsheet models easy

> **Key technique:**
> - **Spreadsheet modelling**
>
> **Fundamental principle:**
> **Modelling is a powerful analytical tool that isn't as hard as you may think.**

What is modelling?

Modelling is a form of data analysis (usually in spreadsheet programs like Microsoft Excel) where forecasts are made based on a set of input data and assumptions. Whilst modelling is full of unhelpful jargonistic terms like 'calibration', 'triangulation' and 'quality assurance' which may make it seem daunting, don't let the terminology fool you. Provided you follow the simple modelling rules set out in this chapter, anyone can make a solid and insightful model, regardless of whether they can talk the cant of modelling or not.

Firstly, to understand modelling we need to understand what data analysis is. There are two types of data analysis – drill-down and modelling. There are plenty of books and internet resources on drill-down analysis (see *Further reading and references* and *Chapter 9* for more on this type of analysis), however modelling is often less well explained, hence it is covered here. Table 4.5 shows the differences between these two types of data analysis.

Table 4.5 Types of data analysis

Analysis type	Descriptions	Answers questions like…	Examples	+ve	-ve
Drill-down	Static	How many were there?	What were the sales for Q1?	Simple to perform	Cannot perform complex projections
	Historical	What was the average?	What was the median income of our outlets?	Quick	Reliant on base data
	Simple	What trends were there?	What seasonal fluctuations were there?	Easy to interpret	Simplicity can mask important nuances
Modelling	Dynamic	How many will there be?	What sales can we expect next year?	Is dynamic so can be changed easily	Can give misleadingly precise forecasts
	Forecast	What will be the average?	What will future production costs be?	Can perform large calculations	Needs good structuring
	Complex	What trends can we expect?	What return on investment can we expect?	Provides information on different scenarios	Only as accurate as its least accurate assumption

Drill-down analysis is based on historic data and analyses past trends and issues. Whilst its simplicity makes it a powerful and frequently used form of analysis, this can also be a limitation as it cannot make any forecasts about future events. Modelling, on the other hand, is generally more complicated as it uses a combination of historic data and assumptions about the future to make forecasts. Whilst this ability to make predictions about future events makes it a highly desirable form of analysis, you must always remember that the forecasts of your model are only as good as the historic data and assumptions it is based on.

Having understood the different types of data analysis and their limitations, you must then decide whether you wish to perform drill-down analysis or modelling. Don't make models for the sake of it though. They may look pretty and flash, but an unnecessary model based on dodgy assumptions and unreliable input data is no use to anyone. If the model is based on weak assumptions and input data, whatever it churns out will be useless.

How does modelling work?

If you have decided a model will help you in your problem-solving, you then need to adhere to the following five steps:

1 Decide the purpose of the model. Before you even open your spreadsheet program, work out with your team what you want the model to achieve. Is it to understand the future value of your company? Or perhaps you want to know the expected future production demands for a given product under different demand scenarios: low, medium, high? Whatever you choose, make sure the purpose of the model is absolutely clear from the outset.

2 Plan the model. Again, before you even turn on your computer, plan out on some blank paper the model 'schematic' (jargon for plan). Figure 4.4 shows what this should look like. Critical points to note are:

● Each box represents a separate worksheet (or tab) in the spreadsheet file. You will be linking the sheets together by formulae. Doing this makes it easier to check the model for any errors later.

● Work backwards – always start the plan with the output section. By deciding on the desired outputs for the model first it is much more straightforward to plan what data you need and what calculations will happen in the engine.

● The assumptions section should be the 'dynamic' part of the model. In other words, if you change any of the assumptions in the scenario forecasts on the assumptions page then the output will change too (provided you have linked the sheets together with formulae).

3 Understand the data. The quality of your outputs will be entirely dependent on the quality of the input data. Therefore it is vital to understand the limitations of the data and any issues you need to address with it. For instance, if the input data you are using is based on estimated (rather than actual) outturn for the year, then your output will be the product of an

Figure 4.4 Example of a simple schematic for a scenario forecast model

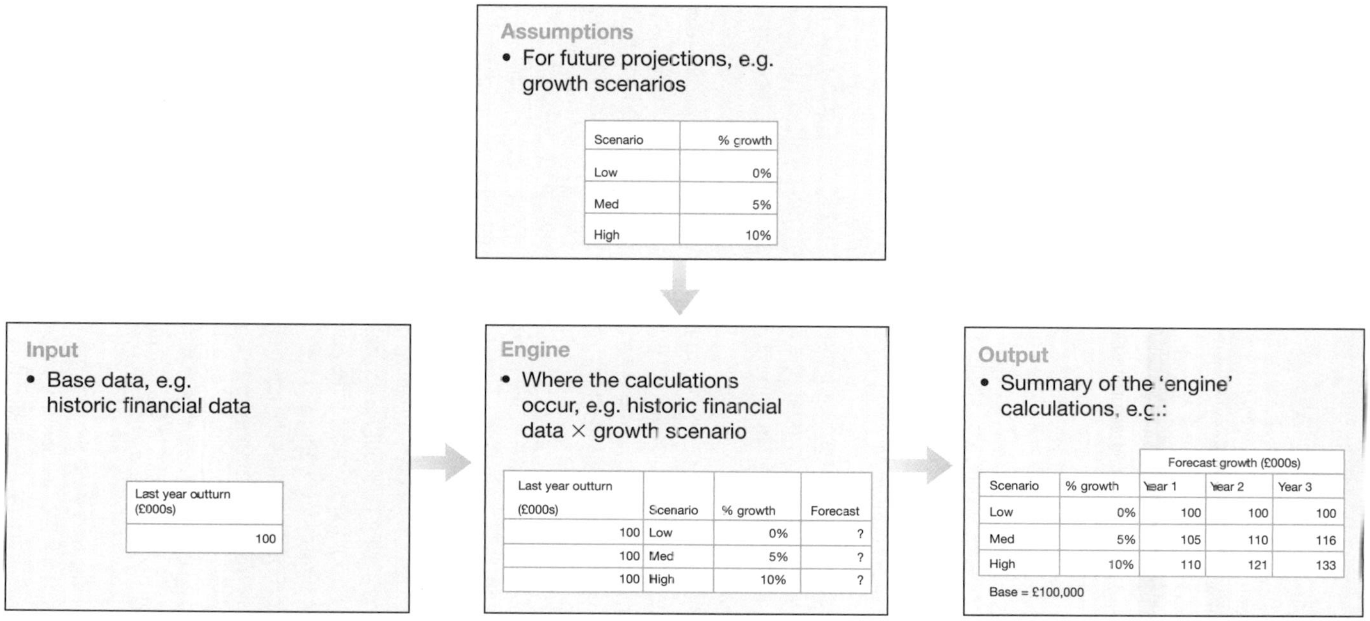

Assumptions

- For future projections, e.g. growth scenarios

Scenario	% growth
Low	0%
Med	5%
High	10%

Input

- Base data, e.g. historic financial data

Last year outturn (£000s)
100

Engine

- Where the calculations occur, e.g. historic financial data × growth scenario

Last year outturn (£000s)		Scenario	% growth	Forecast
100		Low	0%	?
100		Med	5%	?
100		High	10%	?

Output

- Summary of the 'engine' calculations, e.g.:

Scenario	% growth	Forecast growth (£000s)		
		Year 1	Year 2	Year 3
Low	0%	100	100	100
Med	5%	105	110	116
High	10%	110	121	133

Base = £100,000

estimate and an assumption. Whilst this may be useful to give you a 'ball-park' figure, it is hardly robust and you should be very explicit about this when using the outputs of your model in your analysis.

4 Check your assumptions. The quality of your outputs is also dependent on the quality of your assumptions. Again, it is important here to check with someone (a key stakeholder perhaps) that your assumptions are sensible. For example, you may think a forecast growth scenario of 1% is very conservative, but if growth has been negative for the past few years then it may in fact be unrealistically bullish. Context and understanding are therefore crucial in ensuring sensible assumptions.

5 When making your model, follow the golden rules of data modelling:

- Except on the assumptions page, all active cells in your model should be linked together by formulae. Never hard code (type in numbers) – this will stop your model from being dynamic and easily changeable.

- Always explain your assumptions, data sources, and how to use the model on the first worksheet of the model. This is known as the 'cover sheet'.

- Work on the basis that someone else might have to take over the building of your model at a moment's notice. This means that you need to be absolutely clear in your structuring and explanations of how the model works.

- Check the output figures that your model displays. Do they seem sensible? If not, check all your workings and formulae to see if you've made a mistake. It's easy to get carried away with the building of the model and forget the main purpose: credible and insightful forecasts.

When should you use data modelling?

Models can be time-consuming and as such, you should create one only if you are sure it will be worthwhile. In the OBTAIN problem-solving process this means you should already have a hypothesis about how to solve your problem (*Chapter 3*) and therefore may want to create a model to test it. For instance, let's say your hypothesis is 'we should stop production of the Buddy Bear toy because it is becoming unprofitable'. You may want to test this hypothesis by modelling different scenarios of production and cost levels for the Buddy Bear. Once you have completed your modelling, you should then update your hypothesis – stating whether the modelling confirms or disproves it.

How should you use data modelling?

Data modelling can be a very personal enterprise. If you ask two expert modellers to create a model for a given purpose, it is highly unlikely that they will come up with identical models. As such, it is often best to entrust one team member with the creation of a model, and another one to check (or 'quality assure') the model for any errors and ease of use. Once the model is created, it should always be user-friendly enough so that other team members can use it too. And, of course, the outputs from the model should be shared with the rest of the team so that the team's hypothesis can be updated.

Example Selene runs a company which produces hand-painted Russian nesting dolls. She has recently read some industry reports highlighting the increases in production costs of these dolls, and is now worried that her profit margins will decrease. Selene decides that a data model will help her understand the implications of the changes to these production costs. The production costs include: labour; materials (paint, wood); and factory rent. She determines that the purpose of the model is to be able to tweak the production cost increases to understand different potential scenarios and their subsequent impact on cost. She then sketches out a model schematic on some blank paper, including the expected cells, as in Figure 4.5 (overleaf).

Continuing the five-step data modelling process, Selene checks for any issues with the historic cost data. As they were from her company's cost ledger data she is confident that the data is correct. With the assumptions, however, she is less sure as these are industry projections for Central European costs, whereas her production occurs only in Eastern Europe. Consequently, she

Figure 4.6 Selene's model cover sheet

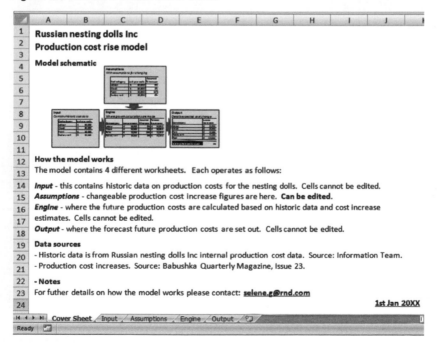

Figure 4.5 Selene's Russian nesting doll production cost model

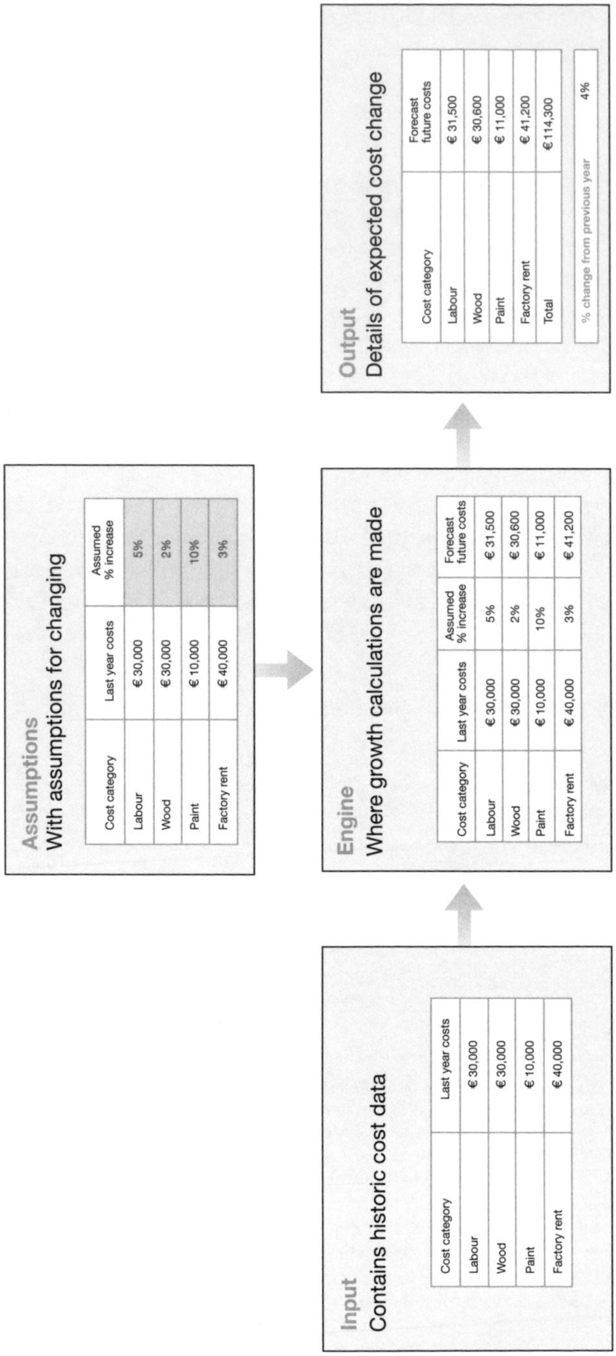

Input
Contains historic cost data

Cost category	Last year costs
Labour	€ 30,000
Wood	€ 30,000
Paint	€ 10,000
Factory rent	€ 40,000

Assumptions
With assumptions for changing

Cost category	Last year costs	Assumed % increase
Labour	€ 30,000	5%
Wood	€ 30,000	2%
Paint	€ 10,000	10%
Factory rent	€ 40,000	3%

Engine
Where growth calculations are made

Cost category	Last year costs	Assumed % increase	Forecast future costs
Labour	€ 30,000	5%	€ 31,500
Wood	€ 30,000	2%	€ 30,600
Paint	€ 10,000	10%	€ 11,000
Factory rent	€ 40,000	3%	€ 41,200

Output
Details of expected cost change

Cost category	Forecast future costs
Labour	€ 31,500
Wood	€ 30,600
Paint	€ 11,000
Factory rent	€ 41,200
Total	€ 114,300
% change from previous year	4%

has made the cost increases *variables* – which can be easily changed – in her model, so that if she comes across new information she just needs to update the assumptions page and the outputs will change. Happy with this planning, she then creates the model in a spreadsheet program.

Selene then writes a cover sheet for the model so that she can hand it over to one of her colleagues to use (Figure 4.6, page 69).

The findings from Selene's model suggest that according to industry information, production costs will increase substantially for her Russian nesting dolls. She uses this new information to support her initial hypothesis (*Chapter 3*) that 'increased revenues are necessary to meet future production cost rises'. Thanks to her model, she now has robust quantitative analysis to support her hypothesis.

Tips and tricks

- To make your model user-friendly you can colour code different parts of it. For example, on the assumptions sheet, if you want someone to be able to change the value in a particular cell you may wish to colour it differently to the rest of the cells.

- Sometimes you may want to stop people from editing certain parts of the model – in particular the engine sheet. In most spreadsheet programs there is the option to password protect or lock selected sheets or cells from editing.

- In order to make the model easy to understand for a user you can insert the model schematic as an image on the cover sheet of the model. This will help to explain what function each sheet performs and how they are linked together.

- Always make a log of any assumptions, calculations and formulae that you use in the model – this makes it much easier to check for errors.

- As you gain insights from your analysis, ask yourself: 'So what is the implication of this analysis?' You may often come up with an interesting finding, but is there still room to dig deeper and analyse further? Even if it means extra work for yourself, keep digging until you know exactly what your analysis is telling you.

Summary

- Data modelling is a powerful analytical tool. It allows you to create future forecasts based on historical data and assumptions.

- Data modelling is a form of data analysis that is distinct from drill-down analysis. Drill-down analysis is focused on understanding historic trends or issues, whereas data modelling looks at future events.

- Modelling is not an end in itself. You should build a model only if you think it will provide you with useful analysis to supplement your hypothesis about how to solve the problem at hand.
- Good modelling is all about structure and planning. This involves a five-step process:
  1 Decide the purpose of the model.
  2 Plan the model.
  3 Understand the data.
  4 Check your assumptions.
  5 Structure your model with care by following the 'golden rules' of modelling.

Did you know?

The term *computer* was first coined in the early seventeenth century, referring to a person who carried out mathematical calculations. It was only in the twentieth century that the word took on its more common, current meaning of a calculating machine, even though the Cambridge University academic Charles Babbage had created plans for a proto-programmable computer as early as the 1820s. However, the first counting devices were *tally sticks*, dating from 35,000 B.C. The oldest known tally stick is known as the Lembobo bone, and was made from a baboon's fibula.

End of ANALYSE stage checklist

By this point in the OBTAIN problem-solving process you should have:
- **identified who the data holders are and collected the data from them**
- **interviewed all relevant individuals and thanked them for their time**
- **consulted experts for their insights on your problem**
- **determined the root cause of your problem through a 5 whys analysis**
- **if appropriate, created a spreadsheet model to forecast future scenarios**
- **used the outputs of your analysis to refine, discard or confirm your hypothesis.**

Checkpoint: Interim presentation and report to stakeholders

You should now be clear on the root cause of your problem and have a good idea of how you are going to approach solving it. Now you must update your stakeholders on your progress so far. You can do this through both an interim presentation and an interim report to your stakeholders. Remember that if your stakeholders aren't engaged, they are highly unlikely to implement your recommended solution. See *Chapter 6* for more on report writing and creating presentations.

Imagine the solution

5

Purpose of the IMAGINE stage:

To devise the optimal solution for your problem and plan for its implementation.

Tools and techniques covered:

- Arrange-Brainstorm-Choose (ABC) solutions generation process
- Incentive equilibrium model

Supplementary tools referred to in this chapter are available in *Chapter 9*.

Key outcomes:

- Optimal solution chosen with wide stakeholder agreement.
- Implementation plan devised for solution.

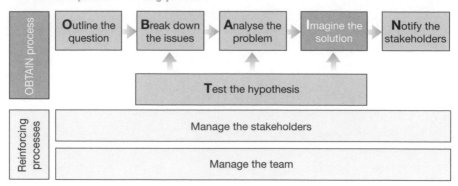

5.1 Devising the optimal solution

Key technique:

● Arrange-Brainstorm-Choose (ABC) solutions generation process

Fundamental principle:

Coming up with the optimal solution is as easy as ABC.

What is the ABC solutions generation process?

It's tempting to think that once you've gathered your data, conducted your analysis, and come up with a robust hypothesis, the solution to your problem will be glaringly obvious. Sadly, this is not always the case. In fact, choosing a solution is often the hardest part of the problem-solving process. There are usually many competing ideas (potential solutions), each with their own pros and cons and with different stakeholders championing them.

Therefore you need to plan for your solutions generation *before* you have come up with any ideas for how to solve your problem. This involves selecting a set of objective evaluation criteria early on, getting as many people involved in the ideas generation process as possible, and choosing the optimal solution (from the generated ideas) based solely on the agreed evaluation criteria. This process is summarised in Figure 5.1.

How does the ABC solutions generation process work?

This three-stage process works as follows:

A: Arrange

● **Set a clear goal** or target that the optimal solution has to achieve. This should be based on your earlier analysis and hypothesis. This target could be

Figure 5.1 ABC solutions generation process

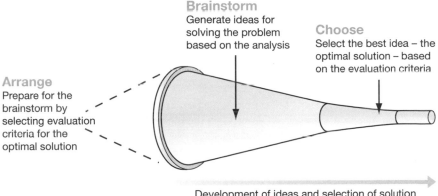

Brainstorm
Generate ideas for
solving the problem
based on the analysis

Choose
Select the best idea – the
optimal solution – based
on the evaluation criteria

Arrange
Prepare for the
brainstorm by
selecting evaluation
criteria for the
optimal solution

Development of ideas and selection of solution

the one you initially set in your problem statement (see *Section 1.1*) as your criterion for success. An example of this could be as follows: the problem we are trying to solve is: 'How can we reduce delivery time for our parcels to the West Coast of the United States?' A sensible goal that your solution has to achieve could be: 'Reduce delivery time to the West Coast from an average of seven to five working days, at no extra cost to the customer.'

- **Generate evaluation criteria** for your ideas. In order to give objectivity to the ideas selection, choose a list of criteria that your ideas will be scored against. These can include things like cost, risk, impact, ease of implementation, etc.

- **Inform everyone of the analysis so far.** It is critical that everyone involved in the ideas generation and selection has a good idea of the analysis that has taken place to date in the OBTAIN problem-solving process. This might mean drawing up a quick report (see *Section 6.1* for how to write compelling reports) which outlines the root causes, hypothesis, and analysis relevant to the problem at hand. This should then be circulated to everyone involved in the brainstorming.

B: Brainstorm

- **Encourage lateral thinking.** Once you have made the necessary arrangements prior to the brainstorming session and invited the relevant stakeholders to attend, you should encourage people to be creative in their ideas for potential solutions. To do this, it might be helpful to share with the attendees the 'performance' section of the VCPH pack (see *Section 1.2* for how to complete the VCPH pack) to give them examples of benchmarks.

- **Treat all ideas equally.** In this situation, the maxim that 'there is no such thing as a bad idea' reigns. Even the wildest suggestion might get someone's thought process going so they come up with a great idea.

- **Group like ideas together.** Once you have a set of ideas for the solution, group them together to facilitate the selection process.

(See *Chapter 9 Critical business tools and frameworks* for more on brainstorming.)

C: Choose

- **Score against the set criteria.** Encourage all the members in the brainstorming session (either individually or collectively) to score the different ideas against the pre-arranged evaluation criteria. Once you have done this, one idea should emerge as the clear favourite of the group. This idea is now the 'preferred solution'.
- **Test the logic of your solution with a hypothesis tree.** Once you have your preferred solution, run it through the logical test of the hypothesis tree (see *Chapter 3*). If it stands up to this scrutiny then you have chosen your 'optimal solution'.
- **Add details to the solution.** Once you have your optimal solution, you should test this with stakeholders to both flesh out more details, and make sure they are happy with it (see *Chapter 7* for more on stakeholder communication). You then need to work out how to implement your optimal solution (*Section 5.2*).

When should you use the ABC solutions generation process?

The ideas generation and solution selection process should be undertaken only when a thorough analysis of the problem has been performed. Without this analysis (both quantitative and qualitative), your solution will be based on mere guess-work: nothing more than a 'hunch'. This is completely contrary to the principles of problem-solving: that an optimal solution is grounded in robust analysis. Even once you have come up with a preferred solution, you may feel it is necessary to conduct a bit more analysis so you are 100% sure about the logic of the choice. The need for this should become apparent when testing the preferred solution with a hypothesis tree (*Chapter 3*).

How should you conduct the ABC solutions generation process?

It is important you engage as many representatives as possible from the different stakeholder groups (see *Chapter 7* for more on dealing with stakeholders) in the ideas generation and selection process. This is because the more people are involved, the more ownership they feel over the solution and its implementation. Whilst the arrange stage can be organised by the problem-solving team, the brainstorming and choose stages need to have as wide a membership as possible.

Once a choice has been made as to the optimal solution for the problem at hand, it is then up to the problem-solving team to work out how best to implement it (*Section 5.2*). It is important to note that even though the *theoretical* optimal solution has been chosen, there is still important work to be done around how to make it work in *practice*.

Whilst the ABC solutions generation process recommends inviting numerous stakeholders to join in the ideas generation, it should be noted that this is not the only way to generate ideas. Sometimes it is neither appropriate nor possible to include stakeholders in the ideas generation process. Whether the ideas are generated on your own, by just the problem-solving team, or in a large group of stakeholders, you should not forget a key issue: the ultimate responsibility for the decision made rests with the problem-solving team lead. In other words, even if the ideas generation is collective, the responsibility for the success of the solution is not.

Example Philip runs a university bursary fundraising programme – Future Fundraisers. Nearly half-way through the programme, he is concerned that the amount of money raised to date is well below previous years, as well as industry standards. By following the OBTAIN problem-solving process, he has reached the imagine phase and is convinced from the outputs of the analyse phase that his fundraisers lack motivation and that this – more than any other factor – is the root cause of the low fundraising figures. Keen to solve these motivational problems as quickly as possible, he follows the ABC solutions generation process.

A: Arrange

- Setting a clear goal. Philip sets the goal for the brainstorming session as being: 'Devise a solution to the motivational problems of the fundraisers that will see money raised per fundraiser increase by a minimum of 10%, measured from the implementation of the solution to the end of the fundraising programme.'

- Generate evaluation criteria. Philip decides on three evaluation criteria against which all ideas for improving the motivation of his fundraisers will be scored, assigning weighting to each of them (see Table 5.1).
  Here, Philip has chosen some of the most common ones. Cost – how much financial outlay does the idea necessitate? Ease of implementation – how hard is the idea to put into practice? Impact – how much does the idea directly address the problem? Risk – what are the chances of something going wrong as a result of the proposed solution being implemented?

Table 5.1 Evaluation criteria

Criteria	Importance (1–5)
Cost (5 = least expensive)	3
Ease of implementation (5 = simplest to implement)	5
Impact (5 = most impactful)	5
Risk (5 = least risky)	4

For each of these, Philip decides impact and ease of implementation are of paramount importance in choosing the optimal solution. He is slightly less concerned about cost because his analysis from the VCPH pack (*Section 1.2*) shows there is a significant financial return in improving fundraiser motivation; in other words the financial benefits will outweigh the costs. Risk he rates quite highly at 4 out of 5 because he is concerned that if anything goes drastically wrong there is not much time to rectify it, given they are already half-way through the fundraising programme.

● Inform everyone of the analysis so far. Philip invites five people to attend the brainstorming session (see *Note on group solutions* above) – himself, three of his fundraisers, and a colleague who has not worked on this particular fundraising programme before. The purpose of inviting the last attendee is to get an 'outsider' perspective on the problem. In advance of the session, he distributes a quick summary of his analysis and hypothesis to date, using the hypothesis tree format (see Figure 5.2).

B: Brainstorm

● Think laterally. With the participants of the brainstorming session gathered in a room, Philip sticks up a big sign on the wall which reminds the participants of the problem they are trying to solve: 'How can we motivate people?' He then encourages them to forget about fundraising and the specific circumstances in which they are working. Handing out a few articles which he has chosen on increasing motivation – which he deliberately picks for being about non-fundraising industries – he tells the participants to spend some 15 minutes reading them before starting the brainstorming.

Figure 5.2 Philip's arrange phase hypothesis tree

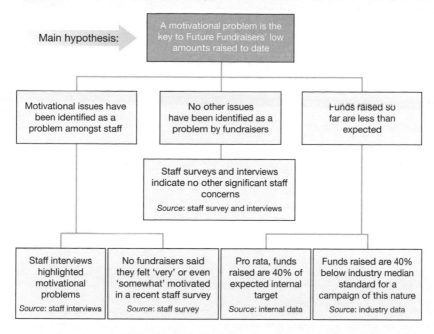

- Treat all ideas equally. Realising that some members of the group are quieter than others, Philip decides that the best way to get everyone's ideas is to ask them to generate ideas individually. Handing each attendee (including himself) three Post-it notes, he asks everyone to write down an idea for improving motivation on each note. He then asks each person to stick their ideas on the wall and read them out. This is what they came up with:

Question: how can we improve staff motivation?

Proposed ideas

Friendlier atmosphere

Longer lunch hours

Financially incentivise fundraising

Better atmosphere/environment

Reward good performance with prizes

Provide career development

Create competition by ranking people by funds raised

Question: how can we improve staff motivation?
Socialise more
Pay people more
Provide career counselling
Shorter working hours
Organise work party
Create performance tables
Less target management
Better pay

- Group like ideas. Noticing that several of the proposed ideas are similar, Philip groups them together as follows:

Question: how can we improve staff motivation?
Proposed ideas (grouped)
Create a friendlier working environment
Shorter working hours
Create financial rewards for performance
Reward good performance with prizes
Rank people by performance
Provide better career guidance
Organise social event
Improve pay
Focus less on fundraising targets

C: Choose

- Score against the criteria. Philip decides that in order to get the input of all attendees, he will ask them to privately score the ideas against the pre-arranged criteria. He then gathers them together and works out the average (mean) scores, which are shown in Table 5.2.
  With one idea – 'Reward good performance with prizes' – ranking at the top, Philip and his group have chosen their preferred solution.

Table 5.2 Evaluation criteria scores

Idea	Average attendee score				Weighted score (multiplied by pre-arranged importance scores – see Table 5.1)				Total score	Rank
	Cost (5 = least expensive)	Ease of implementation (5 = simplest to implement)	Impact (5 = most impactful)	Risk (5 = most risky)	Cost (5 = least expensive)	Ease of implementation (5 = simplest to implement)	Impact (5 = most impactful)	Risk (5 = most risky)		
Reward good performance with prizes	2.8	4.2	4.5	3.5	8.4	21.0	22.5	14.0	65.9	1
Organise social event	4.0	4.5	2.3	4.2	12.0	22.5	11.5	16.8	62.8	2
Rank people by performance	4.2	4.5	3.2	2.6	12.6	22.5	16.0	10.4	61.5	3
Provide better career guidance	4.6	4.2	1.5	4.7	13.8	21.0	7.5	18.8	61.1	4
Improve pay	4.7	3.6	3.7	2.4	14.1	18.0	18.5	9.6	60.2	5
Create a friendlier working environment	3.4	2.7	2.5	4.4	10.2	13.4	12.5	17.6	53.7	6
Focus less on fundraising targets	4.3	3.5	1.6	2.9	12.9	17.5	8.0	11.6	50.0	7
Create financial rewards for performance	2.2	3.1	4.1	1.5	6.6	15.5	20.5	6.0	48.6	8
Shorter working hours	4.3	1.5	2.0	3.8	12.9	7.5	10.0	15.2	45.6	9

Figure 5.3 Checked solution test

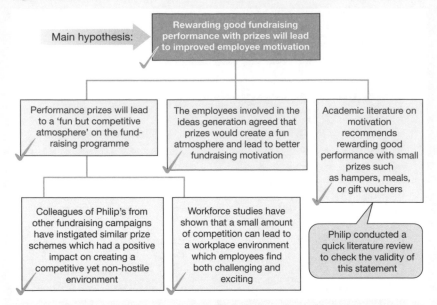

- Check the logic of the solution. Keen to verify that his preferred solution is indeed the optimal solution, Philip performs a further hypothesis tree to check (see Figure 5.3).
  Needing to double-check some academic and workforce literature that he had read as part of creating the VCPH pack (see *Section 1.2*), he is now happy with the logic behind his 'optimal solution'.

- Add details to the solution. Wary of creating an overly competitive environment on the fundraising programme that might have a negative effect on some staff (one of the reasons why 'rank people by performance' had a high risk score was because of this fear), Philip discusses ways of avoiding this with his team. As a result, they suggest that prizes should be:

  - awarded collectively – thus the group receive a prize together for good performance

  - given for 'over-performance' – when the group's raised amount is above target for the week

  - with more emphasis on fun than finance – therefore prizes are more likely to be group meal and drinks (incorporating the second ranked idea about organising a social event), rather than a cheque.

With the optimal solution chosen and tested for its logic and details of how it would operate in practice, Philip is now ready to move onto the next stage of the OBTAIN problem-solving process: making change happen.

- Sometimes you may need multiple solutions to the problem at hand. As long as implementing them is feasible, this is fine.

- To help lateral thinking, run the brainstorming session in a different location to the normal working environment. This could be outside if the weather is good, or at the very least in a different room.

- When coming up with the details for your optimal solution, don't be afraid to merge parts of other popular ideas. For example, if your top ranked idea is to cut expense allowances and your second ranked idea is to publish expenses, these could form part of one optimal solution: expenses retrenchment and transparency.

- Running creative sessions like brainstorming can be difficult to manage. Here are a few tips:

    - Set clear ground rules at the start of the session: mobiles phones off, one person talking at a time, treat all ideas equally, etc.

    - Use a quick ice-breaker to lighten the mood. These don't have to be embarrassing or silly. Just by asking everyone a simple question like 'What's your dream job?' or 'If you could travel back in time to any period in history, which would it be?' you'd be surprised how much more relaxed and open people feel afterwards.

    - If people are talking over each other, try installing rules such as, 'You can only speak by raising your hand' or 'You can only speak whilst you are in possession of the office stapler'. Even just suggesting a rule like this will make people more aware of their behaviour and less likely to act in a disruptive fashion.

    - Often someone will come up with a great thought in a meeting or session that isn't really relevant to what's being discussed. Rather than derail the meeting or ignore the idea altogether, 'park' the idea. To do this, stick a flip chart page on a wall in the room and as the meeting progresses, make sure to explicitly log these 'parked' ideas. Also make sure to leave time at the end of the meeting to discuss them. Think of this as preparing the 'any other business' part of a meeting in advance.

    - Change the topic of discussion if people get too stuck in detail. Brainstorming is all about creativity, imagination, and big ideas. If you notice the group getting stuck on issues of detail, encourage them to move onto another idea. There is a time and a place for fine detail in business, but brainstorming is not it.

For more tips on brainstorming see *Chapter 9*.

Summary

- The solutions generation process is where you use the insight drawn from your analyses to date to come up with an idea that will solve the root cause of your problem.

- To achieve an optimal solution requires careful planning. This involves a three-step process:
  - Arrange – prepare for the brainstorming session by setting a clear goal for your optimal solution, creating evaluation criteria for your ideas, and informing the participants of the brainstorm of your analysis to date.
  - Brainstorm – creativity is the key here. Think beyond your immediate problem and encourage participants to be as imaginative as possible in their ideas. Make sure, however, that the suggested ideas are always based on the insights that your prior analysis has drawn.
  - Choose – by scoring your ideas against the pre-arranged evaluation criteria a preferred solution will emerge. Test the logic of this idea with a hypothesis tree. Once you happy with it, run it by your stakeholders to check they are happy with it and to add details to the solution.
- If you do realise that you need more analysis to be convinced that your solution is indeed 'optimal' then don't panic. Generating solutions can often be an iterative process – don't just push through an idea because you can't be bothered to double-check its logic.
- Remember that an optimal solution is one grounded in fact-based analysis. Anything else is nothing more than a hunch.

Did you know?

In 1907 the famous Victorian polymath Sir Francis Galton noted a fascinating discovery at a county fair. One of the games at the fair was to correctly guess the weight of an ox. Whilst individually very few who guessed the weight of the ox (including several cattle experts) came near to the answer, collectively, the average – in this case the median – of all the guesses of the crowd at the fair was closest to the correct weight. Galton repeated this experiment several times and drew the conclusion that collective wisdom is better than that of individuals (even experts). From this was born a now common business mantra: that we should trust in the 'wisdom of crowds'. Recounting this story before a brainstorming session can help remind people prone to dominating discussions of the potentially detrimental effects of their behaviour.

5.2 Making change happen

Key tool:
- **Incentive equilibrium model**

Fundamental principle:
People are at the heart of any successful change programme. If you want people to change, you need to incentivise them to do so.

What is the incentive equilibrium model?

How often do you see great ideas fail because they were never properly implemented? Or insightful reports filed onto a dusty shelf, their recommendations long forgotten? Or great theoretical solutions with no planning for how they would work in practice?

It is fairly obvious that any solution necessitates change (unless your solution is to maintain the status quo, in which case you probably didn't have a genuine problem in the first place). All the issues above are examples of a failure of change management. There is a whole world of literature on change management – for more on this see *Further reading and references*.

The incentive equilibrium model (Figure 5.4) does not profess to be the answer to all your change management problems, because all issues of change operate under different circumstances and are trying to implement different solutions. But it does focus on a key concept about human nature which is often forgotten when implementing change: that to do something (i.e. to change) it needs to be in our best interests to do so.

How does the incentive equilibrium model work?

The incentive equilibrium model is based around three issues that need to be considered when making change happen.

Figure 5.4 Incentive equilibrium model

+ve incentives

−ve incentives

Incentivisation

'It is in my best interests to do this'

Capability
'I have the ability to do this'

Understanding
'I understand what I need to do'

Incentivisation

There needs to be a balance between positive and negative incentives here. Positive incentives could include:

- leadership recognition and praise of the new behaviour
- rewards (financial or otherwise) for acting in the new way
- tying promotions within the organisation to the desired new methods.

Negative incentives could include:

- leadership admonition of failure to change
- monitoring adherence to new behaviour using performance metrics
- peer pressure.

It's critical to note that disequilibrium of these positive and negative incentives will result in undesirable cultural consequences in your organisation. For instance, if your only method of incentivising people to change is by fining them every time they fail to adhere to the new standards, then you are likely to create a highly negative culture based on fear. Similarly, if your sole method of incentivisation is based on financial reward, this is likely to create a highly individualistic and financially driven culture. There needs to be a healthy balance in your incentive scheme.

Similarly, the methods of incentivisation that you choose should be used consistently but sparingly. For instance, too much leadership recognition (positive incentive) or admonition (negative incentive) will diminish its effectiveness as people get used to it. Likewise, inconsistent and random distribution of rewards will undermine the idea of incentivisation. It needs to be clear how actions lead to rewards or admonitions.

Capability

If you are expecting someone to change their methods of working, you can only do so by first ensuring they have the capability to do what is expected of them. Ensuring that the right capabilities exist in your organisation can be done by:

- training, coaching, and developing people in the necessary skills
- hiring people with the required skills and expertise.

Understanding

You cannot expect change to happen without first articulating what the change is and why it is important. To do this requires good communication *throughout* the organisation. Ways of achieving this include:

- Ensuring that the changes you are implementing are clearly communicated. You need to explain *what* the changes are; *why* they are happening; and *how* they will be enacted.
- Getting a senior executive figure to communicate the changes – a high-profile endorsement unsurprisingly carries great weight in organisations.
- Communicating the changes to everyone, not just those immediately affected. Positive or negative, any change which is not openly discussed will be subject to rumour and liable to create misunderstanding. It is better to control the communication yourself rather than risk the message being confused through gossip in the organisation.

When should you use the incentive equilibrium model?

Once you have selected your optimal solution, you should then start thinking about how to implement the solution effectively. It is at this point that you need to consider the factors that make up the incentive equilibrium model. By this stage in the OBTAIN process you should have a fairly detailed plan for the high-level solution – for example, 'to deal with our temporary profit loss, we need to ask our sales workforce to work at 90% of their salaries for the next two months'. However, you will still not have a detailed plan for how this solution will look in practice.

In this simple example, by considering the factors in the incentive equilibrium model this will help you think about such things as:

- Incentives: Why is it in my interests to accept this temporary salary cut? What will happen if I don't accept the salary cut?
- Capability: Am I able to work at the reduced salary rate as effectively as before?
- Understanding: Why is accepting this salary cut important to the organisation?

How should you use the incentive equilibrium model?

The plan for implementing the solution is the responsibility of the problem-solving team. Whilst it is important to get the thoughts and comments of those involved in the actual implementation process, the detailed plan should be conducted by the team which is dedicated to the success of the solution.

When devising your change factors, look back on the VCPH pack (*Section 1.2*) for any contextual information on the organisation that you need to consider. For instance, if your VCPH findings suggest that the organisation is highly competitive, you should look to implement a solution which works with the grain of this competitiveness and not against it. In short, any successful change plan will complement existing organisation culture identities, not conflict with them.

Once you have considered the necessary elements for successful change, you should then draw up an implementation plan. An implementation plan is essentially just another name for a workplan (as described in *Section 2.2*). It should list the necessary actions to implement your solution, who is responsible for ensuring they happen, and when they need to be done by. Most important, however, is that someone ultimately has ownership of the implementation plan – it is they who must make sure that all the actions are carried out, on time, and by the responsible parties. On some occasions, the implementation plan will need to be drawn up *after* the key decision-makers have signed off on your recommendations. If this is the case, the principle of assigning actions with due dates to people remains.

Example Tom works for the process improvement team at Boffin Model Planes, a manufacturer of miniature replica aircraft. Tom had been tasked with reducing the number of defective and faulty plane parts on the production line, as there has been a recent upsurge in manufacturing error costs. By following the OBTAIN process, Tom was able to ascertain that the root cause of the problem was poor reporting of defective parts by the production line teams. Responsibility for defective parts rested with just one Production Inspector for the whole manufacturing process, and often by the time she noticed there was an issue, many faulty parts had already been made.

Tom's solution to the problem is to create an immediate error reporting problem amongst the production line workforce. His analysis has shown that if a production worker reports a manufacturing error the moment they notice one (staff interviews showed that very few of the workforce reported errors as they did not feel it was their responsibility to do so) this will reduce the number of faulty parts manufactured. This is because the production process can be halted as soon as an error is noted, rather than waiting for the Production Inspector to do her inspection rounds.

In short, Tom wants to use the incentive equilibrium model to help him think through how he can 'create a culture of immediate error reporting in the production line workforce so that manufacturing error costs can be reduced'. Bearing in mind the key principle that people need to be incentivised in order to change, Tom assigns a set of actions to each of the elements of the model (Figure 5.5).

Figure 5.5 Tom's manufacturing error reduction programme incentive plan

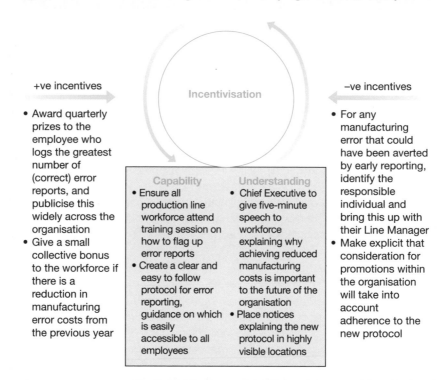

For positive incentives, Tom decides to focus on introducing a rewarding yet competitive element into the workplace through prizes and collective bonuses. For negative incentives, it will be made clear that people will be held to account for any consequences of failing to adhere to the new reporting protocol – Tom first checks that the information for this will be readily available, for instance, that the location of errors is logged and that this can be cross-referenced with the working patterns of employees. A further negative incentive (which also has positive elements) is to make clear to all employees that if they wish to progress to more senior roles in the organisation, they must show themselves to be committed to reducing manufacturing errors.

In terms of ensuring that the capabilities exist to follow the new protocol, Tom does two things. Firstly, he makes sure that everyone is trained up in the necessary reporting techniques via a brief training session. Secondly, he reinforces the lessons from the training by ensuring the error reporting guidance is easily accessible to all employees.

Finally, with regard to understanding, Tom seeks the weight of a senior figure in the organisation – in this case the Chief Executive – to add authority and credibility to his proposed solution by delivering a brief speech to the employees on the new error reduction programme. He also makes it impossible for employees to claim they are unaware of the new procedures by displaying the guidance and rationale for the programme on posters around the production line.

Ready now to deliver his recommendations to the key stakeholders at Boffin Model Planes, Tom decides to draw up a suggested implementation plan for his solution (Table 5.3), assigning responsibilities between himself and his assistant, Will.

Table 5.3 Tom's implementation plan

Task	Due by	Responsible
Prepare protocol guidance on error reporting	05-Jan	Tom
Discuss collective bonus scheme for error reporting with payroll	06-Jan	Tom
Organise error reporting briefing session	06-Jan	Tom
Request Chief Executive time for briefing session	06-Jan	Will
Brief Line Managers on error reporting changes	12-Jan	Tom
Create protocol posters	12-Jan	Tom
Create database for logging error reports	29-Jan	Will
Buy prizes for quarterly error reporting award	29-Jan	Will
Key date: Error reporting briefing session	**01-Feb**	**Tom**

- Poor communication is the enemy of change. Poor communication creates confusion and, in turn, suspicion of change. Make sure to keep all those involved in the change process as well informed of developments as possible.

- Positive incentives don't have to be costly. As long as you can create a culture whereby achieving recognition of good performance is desirable, then the incentives are really just the icing on the cake – peer recognition is the real reward.

- Only create negative incentives that you are willing to follow through on. A negative incentive is a form of contract; if you don't do X, Y will happen to you. If you don't honour this contract, it is likely that you will appear weak and lose credibility in the eyes of others.

Summary

- At the heart of change is human motivation. If people don't feel compelled to do something, then they won't do it. To overcome this barrier, you need to think of ways of incentivising them to change.

- The incentive equilibrium model encourages you to think of four different elements when considering change:
  - positive incentives
  - negative incentives
  - capability
  - understanding.

  Be careful to balance the positive and negative incentives – too much of one or the other is likely to lead to unintended cultural problems in your organisation.

- Always consider the internal characteristics of your organisation when thinking about change. How would you define your organisation: ambitious, laid-back, financially motivated, or with a strong social conscience? Whatever the organisational identity, be sure that your change plan complements rather than contradicts it.

Did you know?

One of the most famous texts on problem-solving was written in 1945 by the Hungarian mathematician George Pólya. Entitled *How to Solve It*, Pólya identified four steps to solving mathematical problems which have had a huge (although largely unacknowledged) impact on all business problem-solving methodologies thereafter. Pólya's four steps are:

1 Understand the problem.

2 Devise a plan.

3 Carry out the plan.

4 Look back on your work and improve it where possible.

If this technique does not work, Pólya advised: 'If you cannot solve a problem, then there is an easier problem you can solve: find it.'

End of IMAGINE stage checklist

By this point in the OBTAIN problem-solving process you should have:

- chosen a solution based on the insights from your analysis
- checked the validity of the solution with a hypothesis tree
- tested the solution with stakeholders
- devised an implementation plan for the solution based on incentivising people to change.

Notify the stakeholders

6

Purpose of the NOTIFY stage:

To inform all stakeholders of your proposed solution.

Tools and techniques covered:

- Report writing
- Creating presentations

Key outcomes:

- Clear, well-written report which details the methodology, findings, solution and implementation plan arising from the OBTAIN process.
- Succinct and evidence-based presentation to key decision-makers which summarises the main points in the report.

Note: the report and presentation are the final outputs of the OBTAIN problem-solving process. They should cohere with each other, and as such it is recommended that a draft report is written first, checked by stakeholders, and then finalised. The presentation should be based on this final report.

The OBTAIN problem-solving process

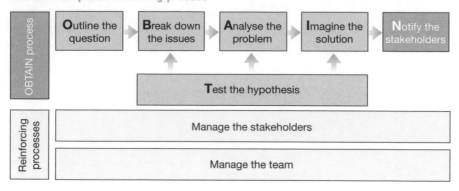

6.1 Writing compelling reports

> **Key technique:**
> ● **Report writing**
>
> **Fundamental principle:**
> No matter how good the content, a badly written report is a bad report.

What is a compelling report?

The vast majority of business reports are uninspiring, confusing and mind-numbingly dull. For some reason people seem to think that elegant structure, fine prose and clear arguments (in short, a compelling report) can only be achieved by literary scholars. But there is no need to settle for the clunky language and unclear logic that dominate business writing. As Figure 6.1 shows, there are six interrelated elements that need to be considered when creating compelling business reports. None of them is complicated and most will be obvious, but by going through each of them we will see how frightfully often they are neglected.

One report, one message

A compelling report has one key message which can be summarised in a single sentence – ideally this message is your proposed optimal solution. This 'one report, one message' rule is a hugely powerful way of ensuring that people quickly grasp what your report is proposing. You can place this key message in prominent positions such as below the main title of the report on the front page, or as the first point of your executive summary (or both). In fact, think of the key message as a mini-executive summary.

Examples of this could be:

Figure 6.1 Elements of a compelling report

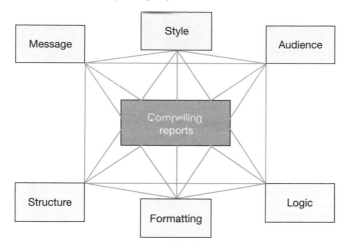

- 'This report recommends that in order to solve our liquidity problem we should liquidate our assets in the Far East by the end of this financial year.'
- 'This report suggests five ways in which we can lower our operating cost base to return to profitability.'
- 'This report shows that our staff retention rates are well above industry standards and suggests three ways in which we can maintain this good performance.'

In other words, the key message of your report should explain three things:

- what the problem is
- what your solution is and
- what the solution will achieve.

To understand why it is so important to have this pithy message you need to think about your audience (see the *Know your audience* section below). The sad reality is that very few people will read your report fully, and those who do will soon forget most of it. If you can catch their attention with a very quick summary of what the report is about, they are more likely to remember the report and more likely to understand it (because they understand the main message). Also they will be more likely to recommend the report to colleagues because they know that it won't be a burden on their time to understand the key message.

If you can't think of how your report boils down into one sentence, ask yourself the following: what is the one thing I want the reader to remember from this report?

Logic – *induce your reasoning*

There are two ways of creating written arguments: through inductive reasoning or deductive reasoning. In business, you should always use inductive reasoning. The rationale for this should become fairly obvious as we look at the two different forms of logical reasoning.

In this example, we will see the differences in deductive and inductive reasoning in answering the question: 'In which country was Sal born?'

Deductive reasoning works by inferring a conclusion from pieces of preceding logic. For example:

Logical proposition 1: Sal was born in the National Hospital + *Logical proposition 2*: The National Hospital is in Rome + *Logical proposition 3*: Rome is in Italy = *Conclusion*: **Sal was born in Italy**.

Written as a statement, this would be:

'Sal was born in the National Hospital; as the National Hospital is in Rome and is in Italy, Sal must have been born in Italy.'

Inductive reasoning works the other way around: you start with a statement and then use supporting logic to prove its validity (note: this is an example of an inductive sentence). In our example, a statement using inductive reasoning would be:

'Sal was born in Italy. He was born in the National Hospital in Rome, which is in Italy.

A hypothesis tree (*Chapter 3*) is just a visual representation of this kind of reasoning. So in the above example, inductive reasoning would look like Figure 6.2.

Figure 6.2 Inductive reasoning (simple example)

Written as a report, this might look like:

Key findings:

1 Sal was born in Italy.

 ● Sal was born in the National Hospital.

 ● The National Hospital is in Rome.

 ● Rome is in Italy.

Thus whilst deductive reasoning has benefits in clearly laying out the supporting evidence for a particular statement, its drawbacks are that it is very demanding on the reader and is open to attacks on its supporting evidence. Not only must the reader follow through the logic of every single argument to understand the main point, they must also accept every single logical proposition in an argument as being true in order to agree that the conclusions drawn from the propositions are valid. Whilst this logical transparency certainly has its merits, it is not feasible to expect all readers to have the time or inclination to engage in deductive reasoning.

Inductive reasoning, on the other hand, is short, to the point and easy to follow. This is exactly what you want in business writing: a simple yet logical framework. It also meets the needs of time-pressured individuals. Those who need to know only the key points can quickly find the main statements and digest these. Those who want to check the logic and supporting evidence of the statements know exactly where to find them: below the arguments.

To understand why it's important to be able to summarise your report like this we need to think back to our hypothesis trees (*Chapter 3*). A hypothesis tree has a statement of governing logic, and supporting arguments which reinforce this governing statement. In a report, the same rules apply.

Know your audience

As Figure 6.3 shows, there are different audience levels of understanding for a report. What is crucial to remember is that a report has to cover the needs of *all* the recipients of the report.

Figure 6.3 Audience levels of understanding in a report

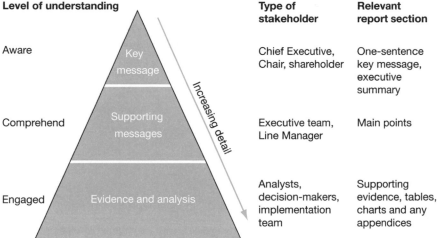

To make it easy for the different audience groups to find their way around the report, you should use simple signposting and clear formatting (see *Formatting is a visual tool* below).

Keep the structure *simple*

Whilst there are no blueprints for written reports that must be adhered to, what is offered below is one way of structuring a report that meets the key criteria of being easy to follow and comprehensive. A simple report layout as shown in the example in this chapter could be as follows:

- front page with title, authors, date and version
- executive summary with key message and Situation-Problem-Question-Resolution (SPQR) (see Figure 6.5) introduction
- main recommendations with dot-dash – another term for bullet points – supporting points (see Figure 6.12 for an example using dot-dash)
- findings with dot-dash supporting points
- proposed next steps for implementation
- appendices of analysis.

Example A report structure: Great North Western Telecoms

Figure 6.4 Front page

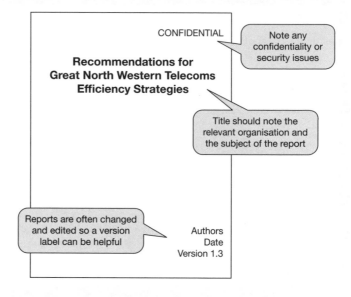

Figure 6.5 Executive summary

Place executive summary at the front of the document

Put the key message as the main headline in the whole document

EXECUTIVE SUMMARY

The solution to the financial problems faced by GNWT is to reduce overheads by merging its two offices

- GNWT experienced a sharp decline in profits due to regulatory changes last year in the telecoms industry which could not be avoided
- This decline in profits has left GNWT operating at a small loss – an unsustainable position
- In the face of this new financial position, GNWT resolved to devise a strategy to return to profitability by the next financial year
- This report proposes a merger of GNWT's two offices to reduce its overheads and return the organisation to profitability

1

Use the executive summary to introduce the key information needed. Here, the bullet points follow the commonly used SPQR framework:

- ***Situation*** (sharp decline in profits)
- ***Problem*** (operating at a loss)
- ***Question*** (how to return to profitability?)
- ***Resolution*** (proposed solution)

Figure 6.6 Contents page

Contents page should be clear and easy to follow

CONTENTS

Executive summary 1

Main recommendations
1. Office merger 3

Findings
2. Financial implications of office merger . 5
3. Staff implications of office merger 7
4. Customer implications of office merger . 9

Next steps
5. Implementation plan 10

Appendix
a. Financial analysis 11
b. Staff surveys 14
c. Customer surveys 15
d. Team composition 16
e. Problem-solving methodology 17

2

Appendices could include summaries of the analysis conducted as part of the OBTAIN process as well as information on the methodology followed

Figure 6.7 Main recommendation

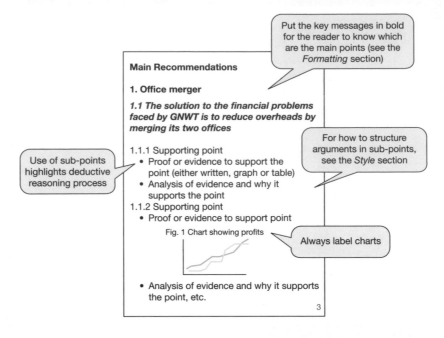

Figure 6.8 Findings

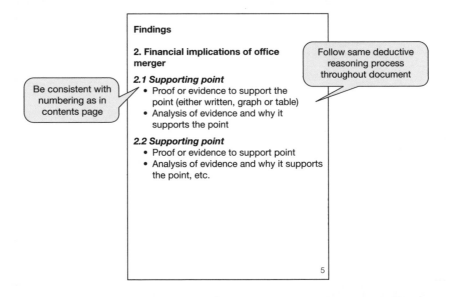

Figure 6.9 Implementation plan

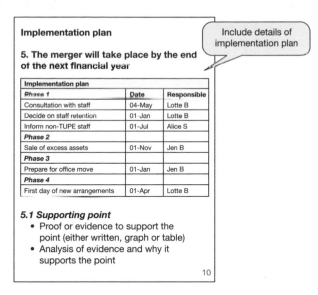

Implementation plan

5. The merger will take place by the end of the next financial year

Include details of implementation plan

Implementation plan		
Phase 1	**Date**	**Responsible**
Consultation with staff	04-May	Lotte B
Decide on staff retention	01-Jan	Lotte B
Inform non-TUPE staff	01-Jul	Alice S
Phase 2		
Sale of excess assets	01-Nov	Jen B
Phase 3		
Prepare for office move	01-Jan	Jen B
Phase 4		
First day of new arrangements	01-Apr	Lotte B

5.1 Supporting point
- Proof or evidence to support the point (either written, graph or table)
- Analysis of evidence and why it supports the point

10

Figure 6.10 Appendix

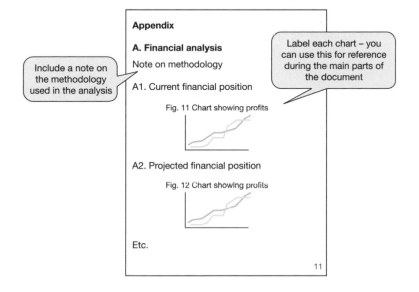

Appendix

A. Financial analysis

Label each chart – you can use this for reference during the main parts of the document

Note on methodology

Include a note on the methodology used in the analysis

A1. Current financial position

Fig. 11 Chart showing profits

A2. Projected financial position

Fig. 12 Chart showing profits

Etc.

11

Formatting *is a visual tool*

Think of formatting (font size, bold, underline, italics, etc.) as a visual tool to help the reader understand your key points. Much like the structure of a report, there are no set rules as to formatting (unless your organisation has a house style), except one: be consistent!

Some examples of helpful formatting are:

- Number all sections and sub-sections. This allows you to refer back to different parts of the document easily.
- Make section headings a larger font size than the rest of the text (known as the body text).
- Embolden your key points (though use this sparingly).
- Use underlining to emphasise a surprising or unexpected part of a point.

And a quick note of caution: be careful when using italics – in some fonts they actually make text harder rather than easier to read. If you want to emphasise something with italics, think about using bold also.

Style – *always back up your points with proof and analysis*

Writing style is probably the element that is most neglected from the numerous books that exist on business writing. These are the key rules you need to remember:

- Every paragraph should follow the point-proof-analysis (PPA) technique (see Figures 6.11 and 6.12).
- Signpost your points. If you have three points backing up your main argument, say this explicitly in the text.
- Each paragraph should have only one point.
- Never use a long word when you could use a shorter one. There is nothing more off-putting than overly flowery language.

Figure 6.11 Example paragraph using point-proof-analysis

Figure 6.12 Example dot-dash paragraph using point-proof-analysis

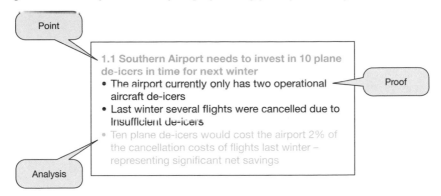

- Aim to use the 15–25 rule for sentence length. A key sentence (for instance, the first sentence in a paragraph) should not be more than 15 words. A supporting sentence can be up to 25 words. This is because it is harder to remember and digest long sentences rather than shorter ones.

The PPA technique is a simple but hugely effective way of ensuring that your arguments are clear, evidence-based and insightful. One way of checking that you are using the PPA technique correctly is to scan through your paragraphs, making a note of the first sentence in each one. If together these sentences form a coherent skeleton of your argument, then you can be confident you are putting the PPA technique to good use.

When should you write reports?

There are at least two reports that should be written during the OBTAIN process: an interim and a final one. The interim report should contain details of the initial hypotheses of the OBTAIN process, and be an opportunity for stakeholders to be updated and informed of developments so far. The final report is one of the last outputs of the problem-solving process and should only be started once you have decided on your optimal solution. This report will contain final recommendations for stakeholders and be much more detailed than the interim report. See Table 6.1.

Table 6.1 Interim vs final reports

	Interim	Final
Purpose	Consult	Inform
Content	• Hypothesis so far • Analysis conducted • Next steps for analysis	• Recommendations • Analysis conducted • Next steps for implementation
Audience	All stakeholders	All stakeholders

The final report is the legacy of all the hard work you have put into solving your problem, and you should not take its creation lightly. As you prepare your report, think of the different elements of the OBTAIN process that you have covered and what your stakeholders would want to know. This should include things such as:

- rationale for the project – *from your problem statement (Section 1.1)*
- findings – *from your analysis (Chapter 4)*
- recommendations – *from your hypothesis tree (Chapter 3)*
- implementation plan – *from your incentive equilibrium model (Section 5.2)*.

You may also want to include in the appendices:

- work undertaken – *from your issue tree (Section 2.1)*
- key stakeholders – *from your stakeholder communication matrix (Section 7.1)*
- team members – *from your Belbin team profile (Section 8.1)*

The final report should be your final analysis and recommendations to your stake-holders. As such, it's a good idea to send a draft report to a number of stakeholders to gather their thoughts and comments. This should be used to revise your report before you publish the final version. Make sure you are happy with the report before presenting it. All the excellent work you have done beforehand will come to nothing if you present it poorly in a rushed final report.

Who should write the reports?

Report writing is usually too big a task to ask just one person to do. Once you have determined the different sections of your report it is wise to divide up responsibilities for its creation. Of course, make sure one person is in overall charge of the document and that it is read from start to finish when put together. Differences in style and tone can be very off-putting for a reader and are prone to occur with multiple authors.

Tips and tricks

- Try not to have more than three main messages. The human brain can only retain a range of two to seven points in its short-term memory. If you're struggling to narrow down your number of points, consider whether some points are actually sub-points of others. For instance, the two points 'we need to reduce staff costs' and 'we need to reduce rent costs' are actually sub-points of the main message: 'we need to reduce costs'.
- Look through a newspaper, book or magazine and check for the type of structure it uses. You'll be sure to see lots of examples of the PPA technique in action.

- Never leave a statement as an assertion, without evidence or proof of its validity. This will undermine your argument, and may lose you the confidence of the reader.
- Always check your report for spelling and grammar. And don't just trust the automatic checker on your word processing program – this can miss some potentially embarrassing mistakes.
- If there are multiple authors of a report, make sure one person is in control of a master copy. Alternatively, there are now online programs where documents can be shared across multiple users.

Summary

- There should be two reports during the OBTAIN process:
  - an interim report – after the first analyses have been conducted
  - a final report – to notify stakeholders of the final recommendations.
- A compelling business report is one which is clearly structured, backed up by evidence-based arguments and easy to navigate.
- The six elements which make up a compelling report are:
  - audience
  - logic
  - structure
  - style
  - formatting
  - message.
- A coherent report is one whose key message can be summarised in one sentence.
- Business writing should be inductive in reasoning. Start with the argument and then back it up.
- All paragraphs should follow the PPA format.

Did you know?

In 1604 Robert Cawdrey published the first modern version of a dictionary entitled *A Table Alphabeticall*. However, it was not until 1762 that Robert Lowth published one of the first texts on the rules of English grammar – *A Short Introduction to English Grammar*. This was not without controversy, as the American Noah Webster published *A Grammatical Institute of the English Language* in 1783, seeking to reappropriate 'American English' from the 'pedantry' of the English aristocracy.

6.2 Making great presentations

> **Key technique:**
> - **Creating presentations**
>
> **Fundamental principle:**
> **There are three elements to a great presentation: what you say, what you show and how you present.**

What makes a great presentation?

Do you ever find yourself checking your watch during a presentation, begging for it to finish? Maybe you cringe when the presenter starts with a 'joke' that no-one finds funny? Or perhaps you struggle to read the words on their slides whilst listening to them at the same time? Problems like these are sadly the norm in presentations. But this needn't be the case. All it takes to put together a great presentation is clarity of thought, an acceptance that less is more, and an ability to empathise with your audience.

In short, a presentation is the delivery of a message to an audience. The audience's experience is determined by three factors, as shown in Figure 6.13. An often forgotten point is that sociologists believe that around 80% of communication is non-verbal; in other words what we see in presentations is often more important than what we hear.

Figure 6.13 Three elements of a presentation

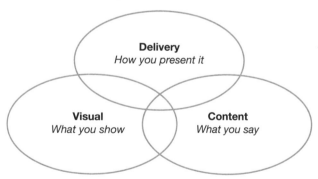

Each of these three elements needs to be planned carefully in advance to ensure a great presentation that is memorable, illuminating and, most importantly, clear.

Visual

Typically in business, a presentation will require supporting slides to guide the audience through the points. Most people get the visual element badly wrong in presentations. They stuff their slides full of facts and information which the audience can barely read, let alone read and listen to the presenter talk at the same time. The key thing to remember is that your slides *support* your presentation, not dominate it. Here are some tips to remember when creating slides:

- Your slides are not a stand-alone report. You will have already written this (see *Section 6.1*), so don't feel that you need to stuff them full of everything you've ever learnt through the problem-solving process.

- Use your slides as a guide for the audience. This helps the audience to remember where you are in your presentation. A contents tracker (see *Creating the story for your presentation* below) can help here.

- Make sure that there is only one message per slide. Use the 'header' part of a slide to describe what this message is – this should be no more than 15 words. If you've done this correctly, all the headers in your presentation should together make a good executive summary of your presentation.

- When using charts, make them clear so it is easy to understand what the message of the chart is (see *A simple slide is a great slide* below). Any chart you put on a slide should not be open to interpretation by the audience – you should be telling them what the chart means.

- Use colour sparingly. There is nothing more off-putting than a garishly multi-coloured presentation.

- Keep the font styles and sizes consistent throughout. The font style should always be the same throughout the slides. The sizes should vary only for different styles of text: slide headers, body text and any chart labels should all be their own consistent sizes. Remember that your font size has to be legible!

- Remember the rule of 6 × 6:
  - no more than six lines of text per slide
  - no more than six words per line.

Creating the story for your presentation

The presentation slides should provide the skeleton of your presentation. As a result it is often helpful to create these first before writing any verbal notes. Much like a written report, think: 'What is the key message I want people to take from this presentation?' (See *Section 6.1* for more on report writing.) The same inductive reasoning used in written reports applies in presentations. You should start with your main recommendation and then back this up with supporting logic – much like a hypothesis tree – and then repeat your recommendation in your conclusion (Figure 6.14).

Creating slides can often be a messy business, especially if your presentation is long and you have dozens of them. A neat way of avoiding these difficulties is to sketch every slide out on a piece of blank paper first, so that you have a clear plan to work towards. This technique is known as 'storyboarding'. A simple example of this is shown in Figure 6.15.

Figure 6.14 Presentation structure derived from a hypothesis tree

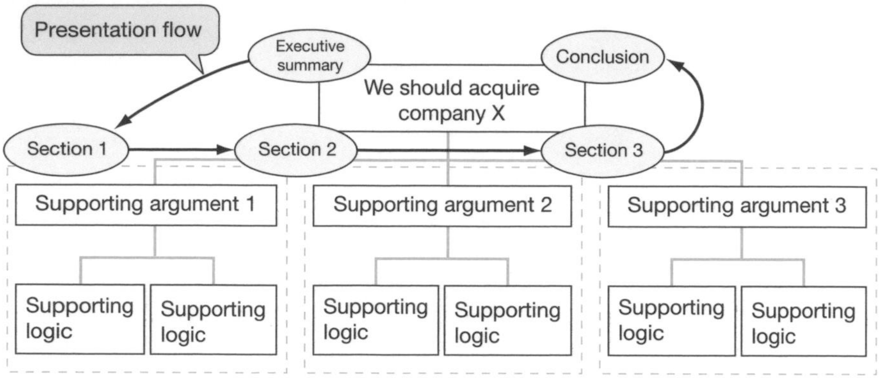

A simple slide is a great slide

You often hear anecdotes in business about slides which contain more words than *War and Peace* or more colours than a kaleidoscope. Whilst the creators of these slides can take some solace in the fact that their slides are memorable, they are so for all the wrong reasons. A great presentation slide should be simple and easy to understand. A great slide therefore has three properties:

1 one message
2 visually compelling
3 analytically insightful.

Let's look at an example of a killer slide (Figure 6.16) and what makes it so.

Figure 6.16 is simple – colour is used only to emphasise the message. The header summarises the single message – if there was no chart, you could still understand the point. And it is evidence-based – from the analysis shown in the chart. There are no fancy graphics and text is kept to the bare minimum.

All your slides should share these same characteristics of being clear, to the point and highlighting just one message.

Content

Like presentations and reports, there are no hard and fast rules to verbal presentations. Below are some helpful techniques to remember when preparing your presentation:

- Make your arguments evidence-based. It goes without saying that all your points should be backed up by facts, but make sure to tell the audience explicitly what this evidence is. If you just make statements without backing them up the audience is likely to start questioning these assertions. Even if you can answer all their questions, the fact that your points are being questioned in the first place will undermine your presentation.

Figure 6.15 Example storyboard

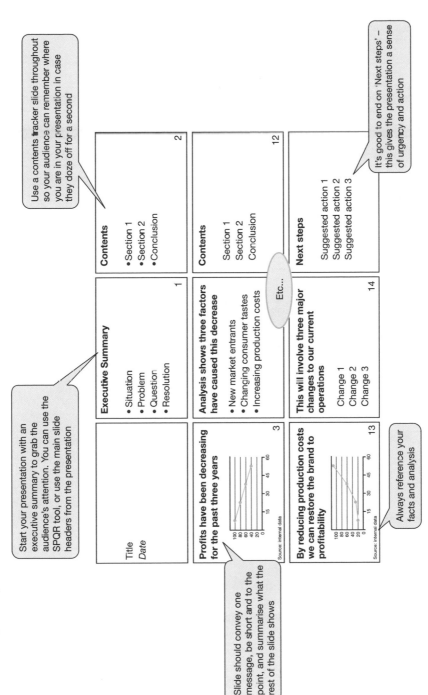

Figure 6.16 A great slide

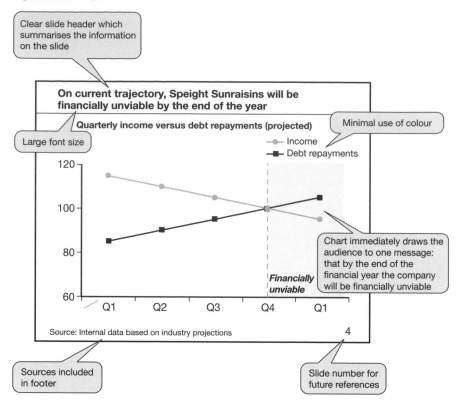

- **Less is more.** Don't cram everything you know into your presentation. Think back to the audience pyramid (see *Know your audience* earlier); a presentation is only going to cover the top two parts of the pyramid. This means you only need to get across the key messages and the supporting points. If someone wants to learn more about the detailed analysis that you conducted as part of the OBTAIN process they can do so in your reports. There are few things more irritating than a presenter telling the audience, 'You don't need to read this slide.' If this is the case, then why is it in the presentation?

- **Understand the audience.** What level of expertise does the audience possess on the presentation topic? If you have a wide range of audience expertise this can be tricky, but as a rule of thumb you should pitch your content to the least well-informed stakeholder in your audience. A 2 × 2 matrix can be helpful here (see *Section 2.2*) in deciding who this might be. For instance, your axes might be 'Level of understanding' vs 'Importance of stakeholder', and this could help to ensure that no important stakeholders are left unclear as to the meaning of your presentation.

- **Choose your viewpoint carefully.** Think about how you want to present an issue when using 'I', 'you' or 'we'. Usually when presenting a solution you will want to create a sense of togetherness and joint venture. Consequently, make sure to use 'we' throughout your presentation. If you tell your audience '"you" need to do this and that', it gives the impression of washing your hands of the practicalities of implementing your recommendations. This can be greatly off-putting for the listener.

- **Make it easy for the listener.** Use your slides to remind the listener where you are in your presentation. Think about your own experiences of listening to presentations. What do you find difficult or helpful? Consider how you can put your experiences into the presentation.

- **Signpost your points.** Repetition here is the key – the more you stress your points, the more likely they are to remember them. Follow the old adage of:
  - Tell the listener what you are about to tell them (do this in your executive summary).
  - Tell them (these are your main points).
  - Tell them what you just told them (recap in your conclusion).

- **Always use notes but never read from a script.** No matter how tempting it may be to give yourself the safety net of a script, this is a sure-fire way of boring your audience senseless. Reading from a script may ensure that you cover all your points but you are likely to do this at the expense of connecting with your audience (see *Delivery* below). Your notes can be as detailed as you feel confident with, but refrain from writing out full sentences.

Delivery

Everyone gets nervous before presentations. Even the greatest public speaker will suffer from the same fears that we all do: what if I make a fool of myself? Do I look silly when I talk? What if I forget what I'm supposed to say? These are all natural and common feelings to have before presentations which no amount of preparation can remove. Good planning, however, can go a long way to minimising, if not completely eradicating, these fears.

Before we go into any detailed advice on delivering presentations, let's reflect on a slightly cynical (but helpful) truth about presentations that should ease some of your fears: *most business presentations are pretty bad.* Though business presentations are usually OK content-wise, more often than not their delivery is pretty dull, unclear and uninspiring. Think back to your own experiences. Can you recall any brilliantly delivered presentations that stick deep in your memory? Probably not. Perhaps your organisation brought in a guest motivational speaker? Maybe theirs was the presentation that stands out as an exception, or perhaps even that one was a bit boring too? The point about the bar for good presentation being low is not that you shouldn't worry about presentations, rather that you shouldn't burden yourself with pressure to deliver a presentation that is sparklingly witty and entertaining. Only a handful of people in the world can achieve this. In other words, aim to deliver a presentation that is clear, insightful and memorable. If you can do this, you will already have delivered a presentation that is better than 99% of business presentations.

Remember that how you deliver a message impacts on how the message is received. If you are hesitant in your delivery, it is likely that the audience will think you lack conviction in your arguments. If you don't look like you are making eye contact with the audience, they will think you have something to hide in your messages.

There is no perfect presentation style. Everyone needs to find a style that they feel comfortable with and that suits them. However, the following tips are divided into the four elements that help in ensuring great presentation delivery: language; voice; body movement; and interaction with the audience.

Language

- **Never use long words** where a short one will suffice. Long words can be distracting for the audience. Remember that your message should be sharp, pithy and memorable.
- **Avoid using jargon where possible.** If some jargon is necessary, always explain what it means the first time you use it.
- **Be considerate of your audience.** For example, if you are speaking to a foreign audience, avoid using words or vernacular which they are unlikely to understand.
- **Avoid hesitant language and verbal tics.** There is nothing more irritating than a presentation riddled with 'like', 'you know', 'perhaps' and other verbal insecurities. These can be hard to eradicate from our diction – we often say them unconsciously in order to fill a space as we think whilst talking. Record yourself giving a presentation and watch out for the word or phrase that you say more than any other. Get rid of it, then try again. These phrases make us sound unsure of ourselves and our arguments.
- **Don't be afraid of silence.** Often presenters feel that every silence has to be filled. In reality, silence (though obviously not for minutes on end) gives the audience time to digest your arguments – make sure to build in brief periods of silence after you deliver a key message.

Voice

- **Project your voice.** The person in the back row of the audience must be able to hear clearly what you are saying. If you're unsure, ask at the start of your presentation if everyone can hear you. Even if you don't feel comfortable speaking loudly, you must raise your voice.
- **Change your pitch and tone.** Prepare for your presentation by thinking about when you should change the pitch and tone of your voice to match what you are talking about. Try linking parts of your presentation to different vocal inflections. For instance, your voice should go up at the end of a sentence which is a question. Gauge audience reactions too and change

your pitch accordingly. If you notice some people looking distracted, raise your voice and project it in their direction: you are trying to engage them.

- **Vary your speaking rate.** A good average speaking rate is about 150 words per minute (this should be slower for audiences where the language that you are speaking is not their first language). However, make sure to speed up and slow down at appropriate moments in your presentation. For example, if you are about to deliver a key message, pause for a moment before doing so.

- **Enunciate your words.** Very simple: speak every syllable clearly. A failure to speak with clarity gives the impression of an unclear mind, and will undermine the content of your presentation. If this careful enunciation feels unnatural, don't worry, because it should: presenting isn't a natural thing to do anyway.

Body movement

- **Stand up.** If you give a presentation sitting down, it projects all the wrong signals: that you are nervous, that you want to hide in the audience, that you are not confident, etc. The simple act of raising your body above the audience makes a huge difference: it says that you are there to be listened to and respected. As you stand, keep your feet firmly planted on the ground and your posture straight. Avoid swaying, leaning or switching from one leg to the other: they will make you (and by association your arguments) look unbalanced. A word of warning though: when you are standing up, make sure not to block the slides you are presenting.

- **Don't wander around the room.** Your audience are not a jury and you are not a high-flying lawyer in an American TV drama. Walking around in your presentation is not only thoroughly distracting for the audience, it also changes the direction of your voice as you face different parts of the room, making your content difficult to follow.

- **Make sure you can make eye contact** with every member of the audience. You don't need to actually make eye contact all the time (in fact, this can be horribly off-putting) but you need to look at the audience throughout your presentation. Vary where you are looking – staring at one particular group will probably make them, and everyone else, feel rather uncomfortable. A trick to help you do this is to prepare a routine for your delivery: look at your notes; look to the back row; look at your notes; look to the audience on the left, etc.

- **Gesticulate to articulate a point.** Most presenters fall between two extremes: never using their hands or flailing their arms around at every moment. Instead, make sure that whilst you do use your hands in a presentation, use them only to emphasise or articulate a point. For instance, if you are telling your audience that you have three points, use three fingers to guide them through each one. If you are showing a slide with a chart highlighting an upward trend, point to the chart and mimic the inclination of the trend with your hands.

- Think about how you want to interact with your audience. Do you want to take questions during your presentation or at the end? In most circumstances, it is recommended to take questions at the end of a presentation and to say this explicitly to the audience at the start. However, if you do this, try to create a presentation which pre-empts and deals with the obvious questions that could be asked in the actual presentation content. An audience that is dying to ask a question and wondering about your response during your presentation is likely to be an audience that is not paying you their full attention.

And finally ...

As you prepare for your presentation, first think about good and bad presentations you have attended. What made them so and are there any lessons you can learn from them? Secondly, try recording yourself delivering a practice presentation and playing it back to yourself. This is a quick and easy way to get a sense of your strengths and weaknesses in presenting without having to ask a friend first. As you gain more confidence, you can then ask a friend or colleague to watch your presentation. Ask them how they felt as you delivered the presentation. Was the message clear? Were they bored or excited? Did the delivery match the content and slides? Alter your delivery according to this feedback.

When should you give presentations?

Presentations can be given at any point in the problem-solving process. They are designed to keep stakeholders up-to-date and informed on developments. It is best practice to include at least three presentations in the OBTAIN process:

1 after you have **O**utlined the problem
2 after the first set of **A**nalyses
3 when you are ready to **N**otify all stakeholders of the solution.

Each presentation will contain increasing degrees of detail and certainty about the solution to the problem at hand. The final presentation (in the notify stage) will be the most detailed of all presentations (see Table 6.2).

How should you make presentations?

Presentations need to be both created and delivered. Creation of presentations can be shared amongst the problem-solving team. This is why it is useful to divide up the presentation into different sections. It is recommended to give ownership of the different sections to those who were most closely involved in each section. For instance, if the first section of the presentation is about findings from staff interviews, and the second section is about financial forecasts, it is advisable to ask the team members who were responsible for the staff interviews or the financial modelling to write the presentation parts for their analysis. In other words, ask the team members to write the sections that they worked on.

Table 6.2 Three presentations during the OBTAIN process

	Preliminary	*Interim*	*Final*
Purpose	Consult	Consult	Inform
Content	• What the problem is • Who the stakeholders are • Next steps for analysis	• Hypothesis so far • Analysis conducted • Next steps for analysis	• Recommendations • Analysis conducted • Next steps for implementation
Audience (suggested)	Key decision-makers only	Representatives from all stakeholder groups	Representatives from all stakeholder groups

There are different schools of thoughts about multiple presenters delivering a presentation. Generally, it is ill-advised to have more than one presenter. The presenter should be the head of the problem-solving team. They are ultimately responsible for the outputs of the problem-solving process, and as such they should be prepared to deliver these outputs to the stakeholders.

Summary

● There should be three presentations to stakeholders during the OBTAIN process:
  ● after the **O**utline is determined
  ● after the first set of **A**nalyses
  ● during the **N**otification stage.
● Great presentations comprise three elements, each of which needs to be carefully planned in advance:
  ● content (what you say)
  ● visual (what you show)
  ● delivery (how you present).
● A presentation which is easy to follow, has a small number of well-argued messages, and is insightful for the audience is a great presentation.
● Most business presentations are pretty poor. Aim for a presentation that is clear and well-argued, rather than trying to be funny and entertaining. By doing the simple things well you will deliver a great presentation.

Did you know?

PowerPoint was first developed in 1984 by Robert Gaskins and Dennis Austin. Though Microsoft estimates that 30 million PowerPoint business presentations are made globally each day and that it has over half a billion users, it is not without its critics, the most vocal of these being the graphics designer Edward Tufte, who wrote a treatise in 2006 attacking it, stating: '[it] elevates format over content, betraying an attitude of commercialism that turns everything into a sales pitch.' In reply, Robert Gaskins rather surprisingly told the *Wall Street Journal* in 2007: 'A lot of the things Tufte says are true. People often make very bad use of PowerPoint... they just write presentations, which are summaries without the detail [of documents].' In short, be careful when using PowerPoint, and know its limitations.

End of NOTIFY stage checklist

You have now reached the end of the OBTAIN problem-solving process. By this point you should have:

● sent a draft report for a small number of stakeholders to comment on
● revised the draft and delivered a final report to your stakeholders
● delivered a final presentation to key stakeholders summarising the report
● planned for implementation of your solution.

Managing the stakeholders

7

The OBTAIN problem-solving process

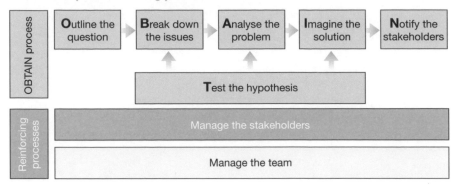

7.1 Understand who your stakeholders are and how to communicate with them

Key techniques:
- **Stakeholder communication**

Fundamental principle:
Understand your stakeholders before communicating with them.

What is stakeholder communication?

Successful problem-solving requires good communication with your stakeholders. No matter how smart or imaginative your solution, if you have not engaged your stakeholders throughout the OBTAIN process your work will have been in vain. Poor stakeholder communication results in:

- unimplemented solutions as stakeholders feel no ownership over them
- misunderstood analysis as findings from the problem-solving process are presented to stakeholders without any prior context
- concerns from stakeholders that the problem-solving team are not doing any work
- fears that the problem-solving team are hiding their work from stakeholders.

Good stakeholder communication is a three-step process, as outlined in Figure 7.1.

How does the stakeholder communication process work?

The three-step stakeholder communication process involves early identification of the stakeholders for your problem, understanding how these stakeholders relate to the problem, and planning for engagement with them.

Figure 7.1 Stakeholder communication process

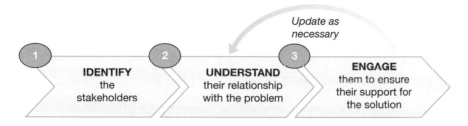

Update as necessary

1 **IDENTIFY** the stakeholders

2 **UNDERSTAND** their relationship with the problem

3 **ENGAGE** them to ensure their support for the solution

1 Identify the stakeholders

In drawing up your problem statement (*Section 1.1*) you were asked to note who the 'key decision-makers' are for your problem. The aim of this was to highlight the small number of individuals who are ultimately responsible for the successful implementation of the solution to your problem. However, there are many more 'stakeholders' – defined as individuals with an interest in the successful solving of your problem – who should not be neglected, as they can play an important role in the OBTAIN process. See point 2 (below) for more on how they can help.

Set aside some time with your problem-solving team to list all the stakeholders relevant to your problem. The PESTEL framework (see *Chapter 9*) can help you identify the different stakeholder groups that relate to your problem. For instance, thinking about 'environmental' groups, if your 'what problem are we solving?' question is 'should our organisation diversify its product base into organic foodstuffs?' then you may want to include environmental group stakeholders such as organic food campaigners in your list. These groups have a vested interest in your organisation diversifying into organic foods, and you may wish to consult them as part of the OBTAIN process. Once you have listed all your stakeholders, gather them into similar groupings – this will help simplify your communication plan – point 3 (below).

2 Understand their relationship with the problem

Once you have grouped your stakeholders, use a 2 × 2 matrix (see *Section 2.2* for more on these) to understand how they relate to your problem. Figure 7.2 outlines a suggested matrix for this.

Each of the four groups of stakeholders in Figure 7.2 requires different management. Ultimately, you want the majority of your stakeholders to be either champions or friends. As you cannot easily change your stakeholders' influence within an organisation (or with respect to your problem), you need to focus on building stakeholder support for your work – something you can change. By understanding how much they support your problem-solving efforts and how much influence they have over the problem-solving process, you can best plan for engagement with them.

3 Engage your stakeholders to ensure their support for your solution

The relationship with your stakeholders is a two-way process: you can both expect to give and receive something from each stakeholder. Table 7.1 shows the type of relationship you can expect with each group.

Figure 7.2 Stakeholder relationship matrix

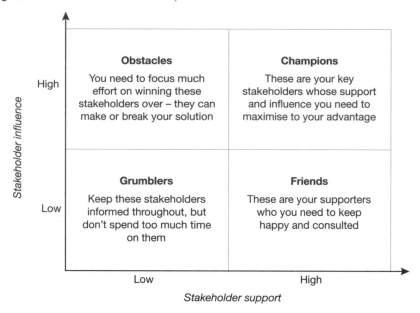

Once you have determined where your stakeholders fit in the matrix, you should use this information to construct a communication plan. This should detail who the stakeholders are, what their relationship to the problem is, how often you need to communicate with them, and what method of communication you should use with them.

Common methods of communication include: email notifications, written reports, presentations or verbal updates. Whatever method you choose should depend on the importance of your stakeholder, your stakeholder's preferred method of communication, the frequency of your communication, and the amount of detail in your communiqué. Take particular care when trying to win over stakeholders who are potential obstacles to moving forward with your work. There will always be a balance here between over-communicating and under-communicating (either of which could annoy them). But remember that if you don't interact even indirectly with an 'obstacle' stakeholder (i.e. by getting someone else who they are on better terms with to communicate with them initially) they are likely to remain an obstacle for ever.

It is advisable to ask your stakeholders how they wish to interact with you. Table 7.2 shows an example stakeholder communication plan for work on how to install a new financial reporting mechanism in an organisation.

In the example in Table 7.2, the Head of the Finance Unit is an 'obstacle' stakeholder. Consequently, it is they who should receive the most frequent and detailed communications from the problem-solving team.

Table 7.1 Stakeholder types

Stakeholder type	Desired effect of engagement	What they need from you	What you need from them
Champions	Maintain as champions	• Regular, scheduled updates on your progress • Kept informed of all key issues and actively consulted on them where appropriate	• Vocal support for your work throughout the organisation (i.e. through informal conversations with colleagues) • Formal backing for your proposed solution (i.e. written endorsement for your final report)
Friends	Maintain as friends	• Regular, scheduled updates on your progress • Kept informed of key issues	• Vocal support for your work through the organisation (i.e. through informal conversations with colleagues)
Obstacles	Become champions	• Very frequent updates on your progress • Regular consultation on key issues	• To engage with your work and offer thoughts and concerns constructively, even if they do not necessarily support its findings
Grumblers	Become friends	• Informed of key developments • Offer of consultation on key issues	• To engage with your work and offer thoughts and concerns constructively when asked

Table 7.2 Example stakeholder communication plan

Stakeholder group	Relationship	Method of communication	Frequency of communication	Most recent communication	Next communication
Chief Executive	Champion	Presentation	Fortnightly	01-Mar	15-Mar
Executive board	Champion	Presentation	Fortnightly	01-Mar	15-Mar
Head of Finance Unit	Obstacle	Presentation and report	Weekly	08-Mar	15-Mar
Workforce	Friend	Presentation	Fortnightly	08-Mar	22-Mar
Other Business Unit heads	Grumbler	Verbal updates	Monthly	01-Mar	29-Mar

When should you use the stakeholder communication process?

Identifying your stakeholders should be one of the first steps in the OBTAIN process, completed around the same time as you create your problem statement and VCPH pack (see *Chapter 1*). Getting a good understanding of who your stakeholders are early on will put you in a strong position as you progress through the problem-solving process.

It is crucial to recognise that stakeholder relationships will change during the OBTAIN process. Ideally, a successful communication plan will increase the level of support from your stakeholders, though of course sometimes other factors may mean the opposite occurs. Regardless, you should repeat the stakeholder relationship matrix analysis as you progress through the problem-solving process. This should be done at the latest when you have sent your interim report and presentation to your stakeholders, or earlier if appropriate. If you decide that the relationship with your stakeholders has changed, you should update your communication plan accordingly. For example, if a stakeholder group moves from being an obstacle to a champion, you may decide that you need to spend less time communicating with them than previously.

Who should engage in stakeholder communication?

There are two issues here: deciding who the stakeholders are and how to communicate with them; and actually communicating with them. The first element – deciding who your stakeholders are and how to engage them – should be a joint exercise conducted by the problem-solving team. This can take the form of an informal brainstorming session. The second part – communicating with the stakeholders – is slightly more complicated. As a rule of thumb, the more senior members of the problem-solving team should communicate with the more influential stakeholders, whereas it is fine for all problem-solving team members to communicate with less influential stakeholders. However, be careful here. If you are trying to win support from sceptical stakeholders, think about how different members of your problem-solving team are perceived by these stakeholders. For instance, if one member of your problem-solving team has a particularly high standing with a stakeholder in the 'obstacle' category, you may wish to try to use this relationship to win over the stakeholder. Conversely, if a stakeholder group for some reason has a bad relationship with a member of your team, you are ill-advised to try to get them to win over these stakeholders.

Example Amber is responsible for overseeing a year-long workforce redesign programme for a regional railway operator – Carter Railways (CR). The programme is likely to involve substantial consultation with workers and unions as many workers are expected to be made redundant as a result. Knowing that good stakeholder communication will be pivotal here to ensure that already tense relationships between stakeholders are not worsened, right at the start of the programme she follows the stakeholder communication process.

Firstly, she gathers her team together and gets them to brainstorm the stakeholders involved in the workforce redesign programme. They come up with a complete list, which they then put into groups (Figure 7.3).

Secondly, once the stakeholders have been appropriately grouped, Amber and her team map them onto the stakeholder relationship matrix as in Figure 7.4.

The group identify customers as having a relatively low level of influence on the outcome of the programme, and as being largely ambivalent about its outcome too. They will only become concerned if customer service is negatively affected (which may become an issue later on). Similarly, Amber's group decide that the Rail Regulator is largely unconcerned with the outcome of the workforce redesign unless the rail service is negatively affected. If the Regulator does become concerned about this and denies approval of the redesign, then this is clearly a big issue for the work, so their level of influence on the programme is rated as being high. The Executive Board (including the Heads of HR, Finance, Business Development, and the Chief Executive) of Carter Railways are identified as 'champions'. This is based on Amber's conversations with these individuals (when she also asked how frequently they would like to be kept informed of developments), and the fact that the redesign programme has the personal approval of the Chief Executive. The non-unionised and unionised workers, however, are noted as being the 'obstacles' to the success of the programme. They have already been very vocal about their disapproval of the programme and its likely redundancies. As a result, Amber's team will have to put much effort into winning the support of this group, or at the very least improving relations with them so industrial action or any disruptions to the rail service are kept to a minimum.

Finally, based on the stakeholder relationship matrix, the team draw up a communication plan for the stakeholders (Table 7.4).

Having identified the 'obstacles', the team decide that the most senior figure in the organisation – the Chief Executive – would be best placed to conduct communications with this stakeholder group, and that communication should be frequent. Consequently, the Carter Railways Executive Board should also be updated frequently, but always in advance of the Chief Executive's communications with the workers (ensuring she has plenty of time to prepare). The Rail Regulator can be updated on a quarterly basis, with a report put together by Amber and her team, however this may need to become more frequent as the programme progresses. Finally, the team decide the customers should be updated on a quarterly basis with press releases sent to the local media and uploaded on the rail operator's website. Happy with the communication plan for the time being, the team agree to revise the plan in three months.

Figure 7.3 Carter Railways (CR) workforce redesign stakeholder list

Stakeholders
CR Chief Executive
CR Executive Team
Rail users (customers)
Non-union employees
CR Head of Business Development
CR Head of Human Resources
CR Head of Finance
Temporary workers (non-union)
Rail Upgrade Workers' Union
Rail Regulation Authority

Stakeholders (grouped)
CR Executive Board
Customers
Non-unionised employees
Workers' unions
Rail Regulator

Figure 7.4 Amber's stakeholder relationship matrix

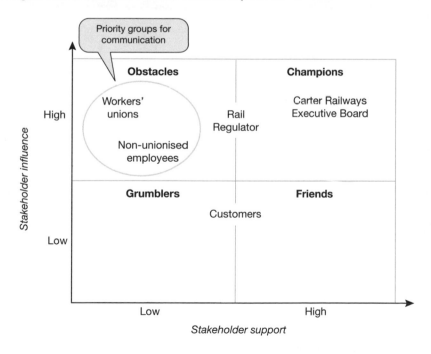

Table 7.4 Workforce redesign communication plan

Stakeholder group	Relationship	Method of communication	Frequency of communication	Most recent communication	Next communication	Responsible
Workers' unions	Obstacle	Presentation and report	Monthly	01-Sep	29-Sep	Chief Executive
Non-unionised employees	Obstacle	Presentation and report	Monthly	01-Sep	29-Sep	Chief Executive
CR Executive Board	Champion	Presentation	Monthly	14-Aug	11-Sep	Amber
Rail Regulator	Obstacle/ Champion	Report	Quarterly	02-Aug	03-Nov	Amber and team
Customers	Grumbler/ Friend	Press release	Quarterly	02-Aug	03-Nov	Amber and team

- Be sensitive when determining the influence your stakeholders have on your problem. This analysis is confidential and should not leave the problem-solving team – a stakeholder finding out that you judge them to have little influence in your organisation can be highly embarrassing.

- Try to identify any potentially beneficial relationships that your team members have with difficult stakeholders and turn these to your advantage.

- Over-communication is always better than under-communication. However, don't send updates just for the sake of them: you should always have something of interest to tell your stakeholders.

- Always be honest when you are communicating with stakeholders. Hiding information or misleading your stakeholders will destroy your credibility with them.

- Remember that without stakeholder commitment to implementing your solution, all your work will have been in vain.

Summary

- Good stakeholder communication requires a three-step process:
  1 Identify who your stakeholders are.
  2 Understand their relationship to the problem.
  3 Engage your stakeholders accordingly.

- You should focus on understanding and engaging your stakeholders right at the start of the OBTAIN process. It is much easier to engage stakeholders at the start rather than half-way through.

- Group your stakeholders by their relationship with the work you are doing. Are they champions, obstacles, friends or grumblers?

- Ask your stakeholders how they wish to be communicated with and how often. Use this information as you draw up your stakeholder communication plan.

- Revise your communication plan as the problem-solving process progresses. Relationships will often change and you need to alter your plans as a result.

Did you know?

The term *stakeholder* has its origins in a legal concept relating to financial gambling. Two parties would bet on the outcome of a given event, and ask a third party to 'hold the stake' placed on the bet, until the outcome was determined. The third party would then hand over this stake to the winner of the bet.

7.2 Trust makes the world go around

> **Key technique:**
> - **Gaining trust**
>
> **Fundamental principle:**
> **Trust is a form of contract between two people.**

What is trust?

Why do some people get picked to do a piece of work over others? Why do some individuals inspire confidence, whereas others make us worry? Why do we feel we can depend on some people but not on others? All of these issues boil down to one thing: trust.

Trust is complicated, but at its core it is two things. Firstly, it is a form of 'trust contract' between two bodies. (The term 'body' is used here because it can refer to an individual, a group of individuals, or an organisation.) One body (the *trustor*) entrusts another body (the *trustee*) to perform a given request. The trustor is making itself vulnerable here: it is reliant on the trustee completing the request. If the trustee completes the request, the trustor will trust the trustee even more than previously. If the trustee fails to complete the request, then the opposite is likely. Trust is built or lost through this contractual process. Figure 7.5 summarises this process.

Figure 7.5 The trust contract

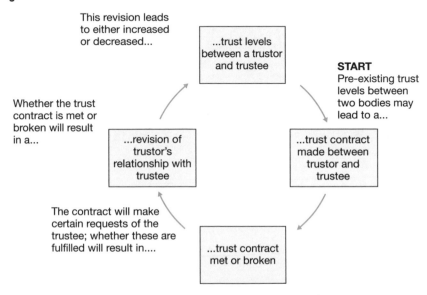

This revision leads to either increased or decreased...

...trust levels between a trustor and trustee

START
Pre-existing trust levels between two bodies may lead to a...

Whether the trust contract is met or broken will result in a...

...revision of trustor's relationship with trustee

...trust contract made between trustor and trustee

The contract will make certain requests of the trustee; whether these are fulfilled will result in....

...trust contract met or broken

Secondly, trust is a feeling that one body has towards another body's ability to fulfil a 'trust contract'. When we say, 'I trust this person' we are exhibiting this form of trust. This feeling is based on our perceptions of the body in question, and it can be broken down into three elements (Figure 7.6). These are whether we trust in the other body's:

- Honourability: will they honour their contract to me and act in my best interests?
- Capability: do they have the ability to complete the contract to a high standard?
- Reliability: will they complete the contract in a timely fashion?

Figure 7.6 The three overlapping elements of trust

Trust is derived from perceptions of our...

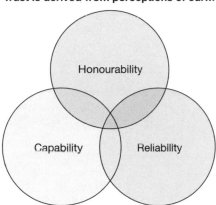

The point about trust being derived from perceptions is important. Perceptions can be acquired either first- or second-hand. For instance, this means that someone can make a judgement on your honourability based on either a past experience with you, or on something they have heard about you from someone else (or both). This is why it is *always* important to act with high levels of the three elements of trust, even if you are not dealing directly with the person whose perceptions you wish to change.

How can we build trust?

To get ahead in business, you need to be trusted. The big projects that may make or break your career will be given to you only if you are trusted to succeed at them. The promotion you've been craving will come only if you are trusted to perform well at the next level. But performing a great problem-solving task alone won't win you trust. Whilst it can certainly help improve how people perceive your capability, you still need to act in an honourable and reliable manner throughout.

Trust can be gained in all manner of environments; it is not just confined to work situations. However, here we will focus on how you (either individually or as the collective problem-solving team) can gain trust through the OBTAIN problem-solving process. To do this, you must follow a three-step process.

1 Understand your stakeholders' trust levels in you
In *Section 2.2* we saw how you can map your stakeholders' relationship to the problem at hand on a 2 × 2 matrix. In a similar vein, do a quick analysis for each of your identified stakeholder groups' trust levels in you, based on the three trust elements: honourability, capability and reliability. Figure 7.7 shows how this might be scored.

Figure 7.7 Trust scorecard

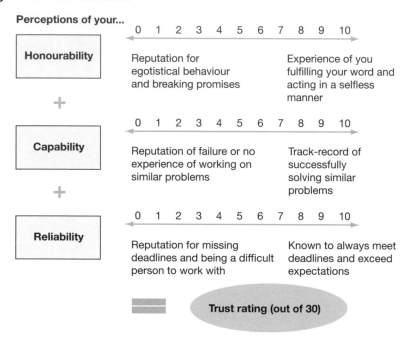

Remember that your stakeholders' perceptions will be based on both their personal experiences with you and anything they may have heard about you from other sources. These perceptions can be difficult to judge so you may need to ask a friendly colleague to help you with this.

2 Recognise the trust contract between you and your stakeholders
For each of your stakeholder groups, understand what expectations they have of you in the problem-solving process. Some of these will be explicit (i.e. interim and final report by set deadlines), whereas others will be unspoken and implicit (i.e. regular verbal updates). It can be tough to understand what these implicit expectations are, and this serves to emphasise the point that where possible you should always discuss with your stakeholders what they expect of you at the start of the OBTAIN process. Where this is not possible, use past stakeholder experiences to

judge what they might reasonably expect. For instance, if you were working on a merger between two public organisation bodies then the general public might be important stakeholders. From previous similar mergers, you might know that the public were consulted at an interim stage of the merger development plans and once a final proposal was made. It would be reasonable for the public to have similar expectations of consultation from your merger. These expectations form the 'trust contract' that you have with your different stakeholder groups.

3 Meet the trust contract expectations

Once you have determined what the different 'trust contracts' are you must fulfil them. However, note that fulfilling the contract is not in itself enough to build trust. The manner in which you do so is important. Think about the three different elements that form trust. If you do not act in a manner that displays each of these to a high degree then you are likely to still lose trust. For instance, even if you deliver a great solution as a result of the OBTAIN process, if it is delivered late (exhibiting unreliability) or if you breach client confidentiality in the process (exhibiting a lack of honour) then you will lose trust.

Finally ...

Whilst there may be some stakeholders you wish particularly to impress – for instance, your line manager or boss – remember that trust is developed through perceptions which can be acquired first- or second-hand. This means that even if your boss develops high regard for your trustworthiness through their personal experience of working with you, this will be undermined if they hear bad things about your trustworthiness through other sources.

When should you try to build trust?

Throughout all business situations you should think carefully about whether people trust you and the types of 'trust contracts' that you hold. With particular regard to the OBTAIN problem-solving process, you should think about how to build trust right from the start of the process. This can be done in tandem with your stakeholder communication planning (*Section 7.1*). You may find it useful to keep a record of your stakeholders and the 'trust contract' that you hold with each of them for reference.

How should you build trust?

Whoever is aiming to build trust (either an individual or a problem-solving team) must act as one body throughout the trust building process. This means that if you want people in your organisation to trust your collective problem-solving team (so that the team is given increasingly important problems to solve in the future, for instance), your team must always work together in building trust. This means that no individuals should seek to further their own interests at the expense of the team, otherwise this will bring into doubt the 'honourability' of the team. If the team cannot look after their own interests, why should they be entrusted to look after someone else's? Of course, if you alone form the problem-solving team this potentially tricky team dynamic will not be present.

Example John has run his own small financial advisory firm for the past 18 months which he set up after leaving a very highly regarded larger advisory firm. In his first year things seemed to be going well; he had a small number of loyal clients who followed him as he moved firms and these clients were happy with the returns his advice was delivering. Though he was never greatly focused on industry performance benchmarks (believing that meeting his clients' goals was more important), he was performing well by these measures. By most accounts, he had developed a good reputation for giving sound and suitable advice.

Midway through his second year, things seem to have stagnated for John. Though he retains his small but loyal client base, despite his best efforts he has failed to gain any significant number of new clients and is becoming increasingly concerned by this. John decides that in order to increase his client numbers, he first needs to understand what the potential trust contract is between himself and his possible clients, and how he is perceived in this regard.

Following the three-step process to build trust, John first thinks about his potential client. What sort of 'trust contract' do they expect him to fulfil if they choose him as their advisor? Thinking back to years ago when he was studying for his qualifications, he remembers reading that a client expects their advisor to provide 'honest and impartial advice that is tailored to suit their needs'. Whilst clients will of course vary in their expectations, John thinks this is still a pretty reasonable definition of the likely 'trust contract' that would occur between himself and his clients.

Secondly, bearing this 'trust contract' definition in mind, John thinks about the three elements that make up trust – honourability, capability and reliability – and how highly he is perceived in each element by potential clients. Focusing on capability first, John is convinced that he has a good reputation in this area. His performance on an industry index level is well above average; he has a track-record of success from working at one of the world's leading financial advisory firms; and his existing clients constantly seem happy with his advice. However, remembering the important issue that trust is about *perceptions*, John admits to himself that though he may be known for being capable with his existing clients, he perhaps could do more to make potential clients aware of his capability. He notes this as being a point of action (see Table 7.5).

Next John thinks about honourability. Whilst he believes his clients know he will always act in their best interests, he has noticed that several of them have commented with some surprise that he receives both an asset-based fee for his services *and* commission, whereas some of his competitors only charge an asset-based fee. Though John justifies this on the grounds that his performance is substantially better than his competitors', he wonders whether this makes potential clients feel uncomfortable and possibly question his honourability. In others words, knowing that John receives an additional fee for financial plans that he brokers (rather than just a fee for his advice), clients might think he will be determined to push them towards riskier plans that are more financially beneficial to him. John notes this as another action point for increasing his trust levels (see Table 7.5).

Lastly, John considers the issue of reliability. In this respect, he has never had any complaints about his ability to provide advice in a timely and professional manner. However, it does make him realise that the updates he gives his clients on their asset performance is done on a quarterly basis, or earlier if his clients contact him and ask him for an update. He wonders whether he should ask his clients earlier on how often they wish to be updated about their financial performance, and update them according to their needs, rather than his. John notes this as a final action point.

As a result of John's analysis of his perceived trust levels, he draws up an action plan for increasing these (Table 7.5).

Table 7.5 John's action plan

	Issue	Action
Honourability	Do clients view charging an asset-based fee and a financial plan commission as being too self-interested?	Model the impact of changing to an asset-based fee-only charging system
Capability	Are potential clients aware of substantial track-record of success?	Publicise expertise more widely: lectures, seminars, newsletters, etc.
Reliability	Are clients updated frequently enough on their financial performance?	Ask new and existing clients how often they would like to be updated and do so according to their needs

For increasing his perceived honourability, John wants to model (see *Section 4.4* for more on spreadsheet modelling) the impact of changing his fee structure on both his client satisfaction levels and his finances. To do this he will need some data on why clients choose financial advisors (from an industry survey) and his own company's financial data (see *Section 4.1* for how to gather data). Regarding capability, John decides that he should put more effort into furthering his brand identity by giving lectures and seminars (as well as some potential advertising such as newsletters) so that his expertise becomes more widely known. For reliability, John considers asking his clients how often they would like to be updated on their finances in future, rather than updating them on a quarterly or need-to-know basis.

Finally, John notes that when he does start to bring in new clients, he should always be upfront with them and ask what they hope to get from his financial advisory services – in other words, determining the 'trust contract' early on. Once this is agreed, he will ensure to meet it, always exhibiting honourability, capability and reliability.

Tips and tricks

- Don't act in a self-centred way. Whilst this sounds obvious, in practice it is very hard to do. People in business are always trying to further their own interests and careers, however if you gain a reputation for this, it is a sure-fire way to make yourself a highly untrustworthy individual. Remember that if someone trusts you they are making themselves vulnerable and dependent on you honouring your 'trust contract' with them: why would they risk you acting in your interests instead of theirs?

- Trust works both ways. Whilst someone is making a request of you when they ask you to fulfil a 'trust contract', you can reasonably expect the *trustor* to help you fulfil this contract, or at the very least, not prove an obstacle to fulfilling it.

- Think of quick wins. Try to identify actions that are simple for you to complete that will help build trust with your stakeholders. This may include fulfilling any quick requests or favours they may ask of you.

Summary

- Trust is two things. Firstly, it is a type of contract between two bodies: fulfilling or breaching this contract changes the level of trust between the two. Secondly, it is a feeling from one body to another that is based on perceptions of three factors:
  - honourability
  - capability
  - reliability.
- In the OBTAIN process, to gain the trust of your stakeholders you need to:
  - understand your stakeholders' pre-existing trust levels in you
  - recognise the trust contract you have with stakeholders
  - meet the requirements of the trust contract.
- Trust is based on how people perceive you. This perception can be based

on first-hand experiences with you, or things about you that they hear from other people. As a result, you should always act in a trustworthy manner, not just with your stakeholders.

Did you know?

The idea that trust makes us vulnerable to the person we are trusting has been at the heart of Western concepts of human nature for millennia. As far back as ancient Greece, the philosopher Plato recounted in *Republic* a conversation between his older brother, Glaucon, and Socrates where they discussed the nature of trust. Glaucon told the story of the shepherd Gyges, who one day found a gold ring which made him invisible. Realising the ring's power, Gyges used it to kill the king, seduce the queen, and take the throne himself. For Glaucon, this story highlighted that the only thing that stops humans from following their own self-interest at the expense of others is the fear of being caught.

7.3 You are the most important stakeholder

> **Key tool:**
> - **Work-life satisfaction assessment**
>
> **Fundamental principle:**
> **Happiness at home and happiness in the workplace are closely interconnected.**

What is work-life satisfaction?

You will spend the majority of your adult life at work. Even the time that you don't physically spend in the office is affected by your work. Do you worry about whether the numbers were right in the report you sent when you put the kids to bed? Do you get anxious about upcoming presentations as you eat your dinner? Or do you just wish that you could stop your phone from receiving work emails when you are with your friends? A bad time at work will inevitably mean a bad time at home. The reverse is true too: if your non-work life is unhappy then this will affect your time at work. The point is that much as we try to avoid it, our working and non-working lives are deeply interconnected. To be satisfied in either we need to treat them both together.

How does the work-life satisfaction assessment work?

The work-life satisfaction assessment (Table 7.6) is a series of statements that is based on the seven most commonly identified areas with which people have dis-satisfaction issues. By breaking down the different issues that make up work-life satisfaction, it makes it easier to identify specific areas for improvement.

Table 7.6 Work-life satisfaction assessment

Element	Time-grouping	Statement	Score from 1 to 10 (10 = highest)		
			How important is this statement to me? (Ideal)	How much do I agree with this statement? (Actual)	Difference between actual and ideal
Profession	Work	I take a great personal satisfaction from the work I do	–	–	–
Career	Work	I am excited by the opportunities that my career holds	–	–	–
Domestic	Life	I find my domestic situation happy and fulfilling	–	–	–
Social	Life	I have strong bonds and relationships with friends	–	–	–
Health	Life	I feel physically and mentally well	–	–	–
Society	Work/Life	I feel proud of the contribution I make to the world around me	–	–	–
Self	Work/Life	I have a strong sense of who I am	–	–	–

Score differences

0+	You are fulfilling these elements of your life
–1 to –2	You should monitor these issues and take remedial action if they get worse
–3 to –4	These issues may require action and you should consider how to address them
–5 or less	Address these issues immediately

To use the assessment, for each statement, score how important this statement is to you (your ideal score) and how true the statement is at the moment for you (your actual score). However, before you complete your actual scores, first try to benchmark (see *Chapter 9*) your experiences in each element against those of friends or colleagues. We sometimes assume that others have it better than us, but the reality can often be very different. The actual score is then subtracted from the ideal score, to give a 'difference score' for each statement. You should then act according to the difference scores. For example, if you score 0 or above for a statement, this means you are fulfilling this element of work-life satisfaction and therefore no remedial action is needed. However, if you score –5 or below for a statement, this suggests you are deeply unsatisfied in a given element of work-life satisfaction and you should take immediate action. Table 7.7 shows suggested actions for each element.

Table 7.7 Example remedial actions for each element

Element	Potential actions to improve each element
Profession	• Look to get new responsibilities at work • Change company or even career
Career	• Gain clarity on the potential career prospects available to you • Understand what is holding you back from new opportunities
Domestic	• Spend more time with the family • Set non-work hours at home
Social	• Spend more time with friends • Go out more often
Health	• Go to the gym • Eat more healthily
Society	• Get involved in community activities • Give to charity
Self	• Make time to reflect on your achievements and successes • Think about what your aspirations are and how you can achieve them

The work-life satisfaction assessment also takes into account the need for a healthy work-life balance. Each element of work-life satisfaction is 'time-grouped' (as shown in Figure 7.8). This grouping describes how time is spent achieving the seven elements that comprise work-life satisfaction. The significance of this is that if you are looking to improve your 'Social' satisfaction, you will most probably need to find time to do this (i.e. spend more time seeing friends). To make this time, it may be that you feel you focus too much on 'Health' or 'Domestic' issues, and so you can shift your energies from these to 'Social' activities. If you did this, you would simply be redistributing how you spend your time on the 'Life time' elements of work-life

Figure 7.8 How the elements are divided into time groupings

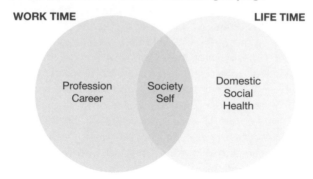

satisfaction. However, you may decide that you want to spend less energy on the 'Work time' elements – 'Profession' (i.e. spend less time working at weekends) and 'Career' (i.e. slow down in that push for a promotion if it means working all hours and having no social life) – to make time for the 'Life time' elements. In other words, change the work-life balance.

Work-life balance is very much down to personal preference – only you can determine its specific composition. Whatever you decide, you must always remember that there should be a balance between the two. Neglecting one to focus on the other will result in work-life dissatisfaction because our working and non-working lives are so intertwined.

Two elements of work-life satisfaction are acquired through both working and non-working activities: satisfaction with our contribution to society ('Society') and our sense of self-identity ('Self'). This means we can improve our satisfaction in these areas through either increasing or decreasing time spent on the 'Work time' or 'Life time' elements of work-life satisfaction.

When should you use the work-life satisfaction assessment?

Whilst it's a good idea to complete the assessment at the start of the OBTAIN process, your work-life satisfaction is something you should consider throughout your career. It's important to take the assessment at regular intervals (quarterly or even monthly) and record your scores in a safe place so you can analyse them for trends or unexpected drops. If you date your scores you can also get a good sense of how you react to different working conditions. For instance, by recording your scores over time, you may notice that your 'Career' scores are highest when you are starting new projects (possibly because you are excited at the prospect of a new working challenge) but lowest midway through long, drawn-out projects. This knowledge will allow you to pre-empt slumps in work-life satisfaction and take action early on. For example, you could ask to be given new responsibilities midway through long projects (such as managing team members or running different work-streams) to keep things fresh and exciting for you.

Work-life satisfaction is a very personal thing. The assessment should therefore be completed privately, with scores being kept by the individual in question, for only them to use and see. However, don't be afraid to share the assessment test with your problem-solving team for them to use if they wish. Don't force them into using it though – it should be up to them whether they wish to or not.

Example Michael works as a Performance Improvement Specialist for an in-house consultancy team for a major online retailer. He has spent the past 10 months working on a process improvement project for the retailer. Michael enjoyed the project hugely in the first eight months, but lately has been feeling burnt out and uninspired, working long hours and spending less time at home with his family than he would like. He has been feeling so dejected that he has even contemplated leaving his job once the project has finished. Hoping to turn the reasons behind his dissatisfaction with his work-life situation into an actionable plan for improvement, Michael completes the work-life assessment as shown in Table 7.8.

Michael scores his domestic situation and professional satisfaction as having the greatest difference between his actual and ideal score (both at -5). Both of these issues need immediate action. For Michael, personal satisfaction from his work is deeply important to him, but at the moment he finds he is getting very little satisfaction from his work. This is because he is finding the work repetitive and little progress is being made in the project. He also rates having a fulfilling domestic situation as being important to him, but the fact that he is unable to spend much time at home (he is away travelling during the week and only returns for the weekend late on Friday evenings) means he is unhappy with his current situation.

He also scores his social and career situations as having difference scores of -1 and -2, respectively. He scores his social life as being somewhat dissatisfied because he is not spending as much time with his friends as he would like. Michael also scores his career situation as being slightly dissatisfied because he is uncertain of what the future holds for him. He resolves to monitor these issues by completing the assessment in a month's time and act on them if they remain with negative scores. The other elements of the work-life assessment (health, society and self) he scores as being fulfilled in and so no remedial action is needed.

Noting the areas for improvement, Michael draws up a plan of action for improving his scores (Table 7.9). For improving his 'profession' scores, he decides to bring the issue to light with the Project Manager, with whom he has a good relationship. He wants to discuss with the Project Manager the possibility of taking on different responsibilities on the project, and specifically ones which he hasn't had much exposure to before (for instance, spending more time interviewing and less time modelling). This way he will gain new skills and face new

Table 7.8 Michael's completed assessment

Element	Time-grouping	Statement	Score from 1 to 10 (10 = highest)		
			How important is this statement to me? (Ideal)	How much do I agree with this statement? (Actual)	Difference between actual and ideal
Profession	Work	I take great personal satisfaction from the work I do	9	4	–5
Career	Work	I am excited by the opportunities that my career holds	7	6	–1
Domestic	Life	I find my domestic situation happy and fulfilling	9	4	–5
Social	Life	I have strong bonds and relationships with friends	8	6	–2
Health	Life	I feel physically and mentally well	8	8	0
Society	Work/Life	I feel proud of the contribution I make to the world around me	7	7	0
Self	Work/Life	I have a strong sense of who I am	8	9	1

Score differences

0+   You are fulfilling these elements of your life

–1 to –2   You should monitor these issues and take remedial action if they get worse

–3 to –4   These issues may require action and you should consider how to address them

–5 or less   Address these issues immediately

challenges in his day-to-day working. He also wants to know when the project will end so he can begin looking forward to a new area to work on, and decides to discuss with his Line Manager the possibility of changing projects as he has already spent a substantial amount of time on his current work.

For improving his 'domestic' scores, Michael decides that he wants to spend less time on 'work' and more time on 'life'. He therefore decides to ask his Project Manager about the possibility of spending more time at home by working remotely from home once a week. He also comes up with a rule to abide by: he will no longer work at weekends. He decides to inform his colleagues of this rule and tell them that they should not expect him to check his emails at weekends (except in exceptional circumstances).

Table 7.9 Michael's work-life improvement plan

Element	Action
Profession	• Set up conversation with Project Manager about changing the focus of current workloads • Gain clarity on when the project will end • Explore possibilities for changing projects with Line Manager
Career	• Monitor scores over next two assessments
Domestic	• Ask Project Manager about the possibility of working remotely from home more often • Set rules that weekends are 'no work' time and ask colleagues to respect this
Social	• Monitor scores over next two assessments
Health	• No action needed
Society	• No action needed
Self	• No action needed

Michael sets a reminder in his calendar to take the assessment at fortnightly intervals. From these future assessments he will judge how effective his actions have been, and whether he needs to take further measures to deal with any other low scores.

Tips and tricks

● Avoid thinking the grass is always greener. We often find ourselves thinking that others have it better than us, but before becoming fixated on this, consider the reality of your situation. You may find that you are a lot better off than you thought.

● Work-life satisfaction can be a very volatile thing. If you notice a particularly marked difference score for a given element, give it a week before redoing the assessment – you may have just caught yourself on an off day. If the score is still low, take remedial action.

● Think about how much of your waking time is spent between 'work' and 'life' activities. It might be helpful to do a time audit for a week or so measuring the hours you spend on each. Does the breakdown between the two look healthy to you?

● Don't just focus on the negatives. If you are fulfilled in elements of work-life satisfaction, recognise your success in achieving this. Far too often people get fixated on negative things without being grateful or happy about the positives.

Summary

● Our working and non-working lives are deeply interconnected. To be happy in either we need to deal with both together.

● Work-life satisfaction is made up of seven elements. The importance of these elements will vary for individuals. The elements are grouped by how we achieve success in them:
  ● profession (work)
  ● career (work)
  ● domestic (life)
  ● social (life)
  ● health (life)
  ● society (work and life)
  ● self (work and life).

● The work-life satisfaction assessment measures the difference between our actual and ideal satisfaction for each of these elements. A large difference for a given element suggests a need to improve satisfaction by spending more time on the element in question.

● To improve our satisfaction in each of these elements we often need to spend less time on one of the other elements. When we choose how to distribute our time across these elements we need to consider our work-life balance.

● We should keep track of our work-life satisfaction throughout our careers. This way we can spot trends or unexpected drops, and we learn more about ourselves and how satisfied we are under different circumstances.

Did you know?

During the rise of the consumer goods industry in the twentieth century, most experts predicted that devices which saved time (such as vacuum cleaners or dishwashers) would be in far greater demand than products which took up time (like televisions and radios). In fact, the reality was quite the opposite: demand for time-using devices far outstripped that of time-saving goods. For example, it only took eight years for 75% of American households to own a radio, whereas it took 34 years for 75% of households to own an electric iron. The economic historian Avna Offer argues that this difference in demand between the goods types was down to how consumers chose to use their leisure time: preferring to increase its quality rather than quantity.

End of manage the stakeholders checklist

Stakeholder management runs throughout the OBTAIN problem-solving process. During the process, you should have:

- identified who your stakeholders are
- understood how your stakeholders relate to the problem at hand
- implemented a communication plan for your stakeholders which kept them engaged, informed and consulted on your progress
- understood the extent to which your stakeholders trust you
- improved trust levels with your stakeholders
- improved your work-life satisfaction.

Managing the team

8

Purpose of managing the team:
To keep your team happy and motivated.

Tools and techniques covered:
- Belbin team roles
- IT-GROW framework
- Giving feedback

Key outcomes:
- Each team member exhibits different characteristics which collectively make a great team.
- All team members feel motivated to achieve their development goals.
- All team members are confident and comfortable in giving and receiving feedback.

The OBTAIN problem-solving process

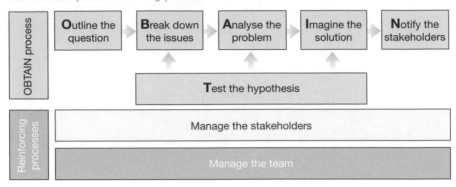

8.1 Setting up the team to ensure success

> **Key technique:**
> ● Belbin team roles
>
> **Fundamental principle:**
> **A successful team must exhibit nine behavioural characteristics.**

What is Belbin team role profiling?

Do you ever wonder why some teams just seem to click whereas others are utterly dysfunctional? Maybe you've worked on these sorts of teams, but haven't been able to put your finger on what causes the success or failure of a team. According to the management theorist Meredith Belbin, successful teams have nine behavioural characteristics or 'team roles'. By working out with your team early on who will own the different team roles, you can ensure that these behaviours are exhibited throughout the OBTAIN process. The nine characteristics are summarised in Table 8.1.

According to Belbin's research, if any of these roles are unfulfilled, the team will not work at its maximum potential. It is therefore imperative to ensure that everyone on the team knows both what the roles are and who is responsible for performing them.

How does Belbin team profiling work?

Gathering your problem-solving team together, you should ask every individual to decide (in conjunction with the problem-solving team lead) which of the nine team roles they believe they are most closely related to. (There is an assessment test to help you do this – for more information see *Further reading and references*.) Once

Table 8.1 Belbin team roles

Team role	Positive characteristics	Must avoid being...
Co-ordinator	Confident, experienced and trusted. Through setting goals, making critical decisions, and delegating workstreams this person will often be seen as the leader of the team.	Over-bearing, bossy or manipulative. The co-ordinator must remember that they are still a team member and need to put in their fair share of work.
Finisher	A perfectionist. The finisher is concerned about always meeting deadlines on time and providing the highest possible quality of end product.	Blowing things out of proportion or making team members overly anxious about their work. The finisher needs to trust in their team.
Implementer	Dependable, effective and hands-on. The implementer is less interested in high-minded theory and more keen on getting things done.	Too conservative in their actions. The implementer trusts what they know and can be unwilling to try new solutions or methods.
Monitor	Keeps track of progress and an eye on the big picture. The monitor has solid judgement and is a dependable presence on the team.	Seen as just the watchman. Whilst the monitor's great skill is in keeping the work connected to the overall strategy, they should not become distanced from the team.
Plant	The creative genius on the team. By thinking outside of the box the plant helps solve difficult problems.	Contrary and aloof. The plant runs the risk of annoying people by not bothering to communicate their ideas to the rest of the team.
Resource investigator	Constantly exploring opportunities and developing contacts. An extroverted and enthusiastic team member.	Labelled as having a short attention span. Resource investigators have a tendency to lose interest and enthusiasm when the going gets tough.
Shaper	Challenges the team to improve. Thrives under pressure. The shaper is a dynamic force on the team.	Inconsiderate of others' feelings. The shaper can sometimes provoke other team members who deal less well with pressure.

Team role	Positive characteristics	Must avoid being...
Specialist	The expert on the team. The specialist possesses valuable knowledge and skills that the team need to harness.	Unable to communicate their knowledge to the rest of the team. Their technical expertise can make them difficult to understand. The team need to make sure that they make the most of the specialist's knowledge.
Teamworker	The friendly face of the team. The teamworker is good with people and at resolving conflicts within the team. Usually quite mild-mannered and diplomatic.	Being seen as too soft. The teamworker's diplomatic nature and willingness to see both sides of the argument may grate with less sensitive team members.

the roles have been decided, the individuals must exhibit the characteristics of the role throughout the problem-solving process. You should ensure that each of the nine team roles is covered by members in your problem-solving team. For instance, the problem-solving team lead could cover all of the co-ordinator, monitor and shaper roles. This would mean that throughout the entirety of the OBTAIN process the team lead must ensure that they demonstrate the positive characteristics of their ascribed Belbin roles (Table 8.1). It is fine for an individual to play multiple team roles or for one role to be performed by multiple individuals. The key thing is that all team roles are covered.

It's important to note that just because someone is ascribed a particular team role this doesn't mean that no other team member is allowed to display attributes of the role too. For example, it would be madness to suggest that because one person on the team is given the 'plant' role then no-one else can think creatively or imaginatively – everyone can (and should) still do this. The point is that in the team dynamic, it is the 'plant's' responsibility to ensure that imaginative and creative thinking occurs. Whether they provide the thinking unilaterally or encourage others to do so too is up to them.

When should you use Belbin team profiling?

The team profiling and role ascription should be done right at the start of the OBTAIN process. Once the team is chosen for the problem-solving process, a kick-off meeting should be set up for the team members to get to know each other. This meeting is a good time to decide who will play the different Belbin roles. Whatever is decided should be recorded by the problem-solving team lead, and they should ensure that the roles are upheld throughout the OBTAIN process.

Example Rosemary is a Regional Director for a chain of gyms and has recently been tasked with merging three of the gyms in her area. She has been granted a team of five people (seconded from the gym's head office) to help her on the project; some of these she knows well, others she has never met before. To get to know her new team and explain the work they will be doing, she sends them an email inviting them to attend a kick-off meeting.

At the meeting, once the team have spent some time getting to know each other, Rosemary introduces the Belbin roles to the team. She explains that all nine of the roles will be covered by different members in the team (some will have to play multiple roles as there are only six people on the team including Rosemary). Once someone has been assigned a role, it is their responsibility to ensure it is fulfilled throughout the OBTAIN process. Rosemary decides to determine the team roles by asking each person to write down a short statement in answer to the question: 'What skills will you bring to this work?' Once everyone has completed this, as a group they will match up the answers with the Belbin team roles. Table 8.2 shows what they came up with.

Table 8.2 Determining team roles

Team member	What skills will you bring to the work?	Belbin role(s)	
Rosemary	Making tough decisions; keeping track of things; previous experience of mergers.	Co-ordinator	Specialist
Carlos	Energy, enthusiasm and efficiency. Always finish things on time and meet deadlines.	Shaper	Monitor
Ita	Coming up with new and imaginative ideas.	Plant	
Mario	Bringing out the best in others; getting on well with others.	Teamworker	Resource investigator
George	Getting stuck into work and getting the job done.	Implementer	
Chandan	Focusing on the detail and making sure it is right.	Finisher	

Initially the team members were apprehensive about answering the question posed. They were worried about either sounding arrogant or getting typecast into a business role. Rosemary stressed that this was a completely non-judgemental exercise and that the answers given wouldn't leave the problem-solving team. She also told the team that they would review the Belbin roles in a month's time both to check whether they were being fulfilled and to allow people to swap roles if they weren't entirely happy with them. Finally, she asked the team to make a note of their role(s) and what behaviours they need to exhibit (Table 8.1) throughout the problem-solving process.

Of all the Belbin roles, 'resource investigator' was the one which Rosemary's team had the most trouble filling. Whilst Mario certainly exhibited many of the extroverted and enthusiastic traits of the role, he was concerned that his relatively junior position would inhibit the networking side of the role. Rosemary encouraged him to take up the role on the basis that they would reassess the situation after the first monthly check. At this point, though Mario had done well, after discussions Rosemary agreed to take over the resource investigator role from him. As a relatively new member of the organisation, it was felt he needed a bit more time and space to get used to his surroundings, and that running two Belbin roles would be a bit too much of a burden. Rosemary, on the other hand, seemed to have some spare capacity as the project was progressing well and she could afford to take a relatively hands-off 'co-ordinator' role.

Tips and tricks

- It's a good idea to get the team members to complete a Self-Perception Inventory (SPI) score to determine which role is best suited to them in advance of the team kick-off meeting. The SPI is available in Meredith Belbin's *Management Teams: Why They Succeed or Fail* (see *Further reading and references*).

- Don't force people into team roles. Sometimes it happens that no-one is a natural fit for a particular team role. If this is the case, you may want to consider changing the composition of your team. If this is not possible, then the next best thing is to make the missing role a team responsibility. Make everyone aware that this is a blind-spot for the team and it is up to the collective to compensate for it.

- Be sensitive when ascribing team roles. Whilst all the team roles have positive characteristics which are vital in constructing a successful team, it can be a sensitive issue deciding who should play what role. Someone might like to see themselves as being the creative mind on a team, whereas the reality is that another team member might more appropriately fill the role. Using an independent scoring test like the SPI can help bring objectivity to choosing the roles.

- If it seems like the Belbin roles aren't working for individuals, don't be afraid to swap role responsibilities between different team members. Doing so can provide a bit of freshness to the problem-solving team.

Summary

- Belbin team profiling is based on research that shows successful teams exhibit nine different behavioural traits which are equivalent to team roles. The nine roles are:
  - co-ordinator
  - finisher
  - implementer
  - monitor
  - plant
  - resource investigator
  - shaper
  - specialist
  - teamworker.
- These nine different team roles should be played by the members of the problem-solving team. It is fine for individuals to play multiple roles, or for more than one person to play the same role. The important thing is to make sure the different roles are adequately covered.
- Once team roles are ascribed, it is the responsibility of the team members to ensure that their particular role behavioural characteristics are apparent throughout the OBTAIN process. The team lead should check at regular intervals throughout the process that this is the case.

Did you know?

One of the earliest research studies on team behavioural dynamics took place at the Hawthorne Works factory near Chicago, where a series of experiments was carried out between 1924 and 1932. The most famous of the findings which emerged from the research is the so-called 'Hawthorne Effect', which suggested a short-term increase in productivity was gained from the motivational effect of displaying an interest in the workers in the factory. Tests were carried out to see if workers' productivity increased when working under higher or lower levels of light. Productivity did indeed increase during the experiment, but decreased once the illumination experiment stopped.

8.2 Helping others reach their goal

Key technique:
- **IT-GROW framework**

Fundamental principle:
Developing people keeps them inspired and motivated.

What is the IT-GROW framework?

Developing people is not something that should be taken lightly. A development relationship can exist between two people: a coach (usually the problem-solving team lead or line manager) and a coachee (usually a problem-solving team member or line managee). However, it is important to note that a development relationship does not always have to exist between a team leader and team members. Before such a relationship is begun, both sides must agree to enter into a development relationship and be fully committed to its success. They should not engage in such a relationship merely out of a sense of duty or obligation. In many ways a development relationship is similar to a trust contract (see *Section 7.2*) between two parties. The coachee trusts the coach to develop them to the best of their abilities, and in the same way the coach trusts the coachee to be as committed to their development as they are.

The IT-GROW framework provides a way of framing a development conversation between a coach and coachee. The aim of the conversation is to get the coachee to understand what development goals they should set themselves during a given time period and how they can achieve them. The technique revolves around a six-step process as summarised in Figure 8.1.

Note that the term 'coach' is used here to describe a person advising or helping another person. It does not mean a fully qualified coach in a professional sense. This is a significant point. Don't get trapped into thinking that only professional coaches can fulfil a development coach role. Good coaching is about *helping the coachee achieve their desired goals*. You don't need years of experience or qualifications to be good at this. A friendly ear, honest intentions, and remembering that coaching is all about the other person, and not about you, is all it takes to lead an effective development relationship.

Figure 8.1 IT-GROW framework

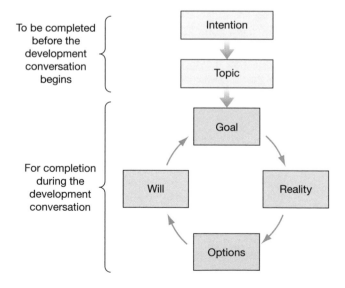

How does the IT-GROW framework work?

Each stage of the framework has a question that both the coach and coachee should answer – these are shown in Table 8.3. The coachee should answer these questions to ensure the conversation is focused on achieving a goal; the coach should answer them to make sure they are always acting in the best interests of the coachee.

Table 8.3 The IT-GROW framework's questions

Stage	Questions both the coach and coachee should ask:
Intention	What are my motivations for beginning this development relationship?
Topic	What topic will the development relationship focus on?
Goal	What is the coachee's goal?
Reality	What is the gap between the coachee's goal and their current situation?
Options	What are the options available for bridging this gap?
Will	How committed is the coachee to meeting this goal?

The first two stages (IT) should be completed as a preliminary part of a development relationship. If the intention and topic for the relationship are not satisfactorily agreed upon by both coach and coachee, then they should not proceed with the IT-GROW framework.

Intention

The first part of the framework is about ensuring that a development relationship is only started from good intentions. Before a development conversation is even begun both the potential coach and coachee should individually ask themselves why they are willing to begin a development relationship. At all times both parties should remember that coaching is about *helping the coachee achieve their desired goals*. If the intentions for starting a coaching relationship are not compatible with this goal then one should not be begun. For example, a line manager may want to use the IT-GROW framework on a line managee with whom they have a fractured relationship. The line manager believes starting this type of development relationship will bring the two closer together and ease the tensions in their relationship. But the line manager is being self-motivated here: they want to coach in order to meet their goal of improving the relationship with their line managee. This is clearly not about *helping the coachee achieve their desired goal*, and so for these reasons, it would be unwise and inappropriate for a development relationship to begin.

Topic

Both parties in the development relationship need to agree on an appropriate topic to work on together. A topic is a general area of development such as interviewing, modelling, time-management or problem-solving. Whilst a coach doesn't have to be an expert in the topic the coachee wants to focus on for development, the coachee may prefer this to be the case. The key point is that both the coach and coachee are happy with the chosen topic and confident in the other's ability to make a success of the development relationship. The topic should be chosen in advance of the first development conversation.

Once the intention and topic have been decided, a development conversation (usually an hour-long meeting between coach and coachee) should be held where the following stages of the framework (GROW) are completed.

Goal

The first part of the development conversation is about understanding what the coachee's goal is. Much like the criteria for success in a problem statement (see *Section 1.1*), the set goal should be 'SMART'. That is:

- **S**pecific – *goal is a definable target*
- **M**easurable – *it is possible to determine whether the goal has been met*
- **A**ctionable – *the goal is feasible*
- **R**elevant – *the goal is relevant to the development topic*
- **T**ime-bound – *there are set deadlines for when the goal needs to be met.*

The coachee must decide on the goal themselves. The role of the coach is to ensure that the goal meets the SMART criteria listed above. Multiple goals can be chosen, but meeting them must be realistic and they must all be relevant to the selected topic.

Reality

Once the goal has been chosen, the conversation should then turn into a gap analysis of the coachee's desired goal and the reality of how far away they are from achieving this. For example, the coachee may set their goal as being: 'I want to use this work to develop my presentation skills so that in six months' time I have delivered at least three presentations to major stakeholders; I currently rate my confidence in delivering presentations at being four out of 10 and in six months' time I want to rate this at eight out of 10 or above.' In this instance the development conversation should be about understanding the coachee's current ability, experience and confidence in delivering presentations. The coach should invite the coachee to self-assess first before offering any comments.

Options

At this stage the different options available to help the coachee meet their goals are discussed. This is similar to drawing up an action plan. Examples of options can include things like: offering to deliver the next presentation that the team has to give; going on a training course; or taking greater project-management responsibilities.

Once these options have been agreed, they should be put into a workplan (see *Section 2.2*) and assigned deadlines.

Will
The final part of the development conversation is about committing the coachee to achieve their goal. The coachee must be completely honest here: if they do not feel fully committed, then the GROW process may need to be started again until the coachee's will rating reaches a satisfactory level. The role of the coach should be to identify possible obstacles to reaching the goal, whilst suggesting ways to overcome them and encouraging the coachee to do so. Once this has been done, the coach and coachee should agree to meet again to monitor the progress made in achieving the goal and fulfilling the discussed options. The GROW framework may again be a useful tool in these subsequent conversations, as the goals are reiterated, reality updated, options checked and reaffirmed. The development relationship should continue until the coachee's goal has been met.

When should you use the IT-GROW framework?

A development relationship should ideally be started at the beginning of the OBTAIN process. This way the coachee's goals can tie into the work done during the problem-solving process. If the coach and coachee are both members of the problem-solving team (and so working on OBTAIN together) it can be a good idea to tie the coachee's goal deadline in with the end of the OBTAIN process. This way there is continuity of timing throughout. Checks on the coachee's progress in reaching their goal should be made throughout the problem-solving process.

How should you use the IT-GROW framework?

The framework is designed for a coach to use with their coachee during a development relationship. However, the principles behind the framework – that to achieve a goal first you need to set a target, understand how far away you are from achieving it, and then plan how to meet it – can be used in all manner of situations and by all members of the problem-solving team.

Example Rob has recently been promoted to Engagement Lead at a global consultancy firm, and as a result now plays the role of Line Manager to his current team of five. It is early on in his current project and Rob is about to have his first Line Manager meeting with a member of his team, Andrew. Andrew has been worrying for some time about this project as he knows he will be responsible for creating a large financial model, and he doesn't feel that he has enough experience in modelling yet. He has already told Rob that he would like to discuss how to improve his modelling skills in their meeting. In

▶

doing so he is clearly stating his motivations for entering into the development conversation.

Before going into the meeting, Rob decides that he will use the IT-GROW framework to help Andrew. First, he asks himself what his *intentions* are in helping Andrew. Rob is fully committed to increasing Andrew's confidence and aptitude at modelling; not only does he enjoy helping people develop, he realises that improving Andrew's modelling skills is important to the success of the project too. Noticing that his motives are not entirely selfless, Rob honestly asks himself: '*Am I committed to ensuring Andrew reaches his desired goals?*' He feels that he genuinely is, and the fact that there is a benefit to the project that Andrew reaches them is just a pleasant coincidence. Confident that his intentions are good, he is happy to proceed to the next part of the framework.

Andrew has already told Rob what *topic* he would like to focus on – data modelling. Rob believes he has enough knowledge and experience in modelling to be useful to Andrew and so is happy for them to discuss this topic.

At the start of the Line Manager meeting Rob explains the IT-GROW framework to Andrew. Having checked that he is happy for them to use it during the conversation, he then asks Andrew what his development *goals* are. After discussing his concerns about his modelling skills and the need to create a financial model during the project, they settle on Andrew's goal as being: '*To increase my confidence in modelling in advance of the major financial model I need to create in two months' time.*' Rob is reasonably happy that this goal meets the SMART criteria (specific; measurable; actionable; relevant; time-bound). However, he would rather that the goal be more objectively measured, so he asks Andrew to score his current confidence out of 10 with a note explaining his score (he scores four). Andrew will re-score his confidence in two months' time with the aim being that he scores it at eight or above.

They then discuss the *reality* of Andrew's current modelling experience and capability. After Rob asks him to list all the modelling work he has done in the past, Andrew realises he actually has quite a significant amount of modelling experience. He went on a half-day modelling training session when he joined the consultancy firm last year, has created two, small, cost-benefit analysis models in the past, and has quality assured another model too. It seems that Andrew's real concerns are about the size and complexity of the model he is expected to make, and the pressure he feels he will be under to make a perfect model. On the latter point, Rob eases his fears by stressing that the responsibility for the final model does not rest with Andrew alone. As the team lead Rob will be there to guide Andrew through the modelling process and offer help whenever he needs it; another team member will quality assure the model before it is finished; and finally Rob points out that the responsibility for the final outputs of the work (of which the model is only one) rests with the whole team, and ultimately the team lead. By stressing the reality of the situation Rob has assuaged one of Andrew's key concerns.

To meet Andrew's goal, it now seems clear that he needs to get experience in creating a larger model than anything he has done before. They discuss different *options* to achieve this and agree on three. First, Andrew will go through his previous modelling training notes and remind himself of the basic principles (described in *Section 4.4*). Second, Rob will send him a series of large models and their schematic plans so he can familiarise himself with what a complex model looks like. And third, Rob agrees to send Andrew on a two-day modelling training course to brush up on his skills. Though the timelines are tight, Rob frees up time in Andrew's schedule so he can complete these three actions over the next two months.

Finally, the two discuss Andrew's *will* to complete the tasks and meet his goal of improved confidence in modelling. Andrew promises that he is fully committed to the goal, and that he will have completed all the actions in two months' time. Rob is happy with the outcome of the meeting, and they set times to meet fortnightly until the two months are up. This way they can monitor Andrew's progress and modify his action plan if necessary.

Tips and tricks

- Arrange for either the coach or coachee to keep a log of the agreed development goals. Without a record of what the goals are there is no way of knowing whether they have been met.
- If you are looking for a coach, think outside of the box. Your coach doesn't have to be someone in your organisation, or even working in your industry; they just need to be someone you trust.
- Gap analysis is a useful tool in business. It is about understanding the reality of the situation compared with the desired future state. You can use it in non-developmental relationships too and you should look to do this.

Summary

- Development relationships exist between a coach and coachee. The coach helps the coachee to understand their development goals and how they can reach them.
- Development relationships are a form of coaching. Coaching is all about *helping the coachee achieve their desired goals*.
- The IT-GROW technique helps to frame a development conversation. The first part of the technique (IT) is about understanding the motivations of the coach and coachee for engaging the development relationship, and then agreeing upon a topic to focus on for development. The second part (GROW) sets goals for development, analyses the gap between the reality

and the goal, lays out the options for reaching the goal, and gauges the coachee's determination to achieve their goal.

- Once a goal has been set, the development relationship should continue until it has been reached. The coachee's progress in achieving their goal should be checked throughout the relationship.

Did you know?

The GROW model (which the IT-GROW framework is based on) comes from tennis. The author and sports coach W. Timothy Gallwey first developed the model when training his tennis coachees. He noticed that giving his coachees direct instructions such as 'Keep your eye on the ball' had only a minimal positive effect on changing their behaviour. As a result, rather than telling his trainees what to do, he began asking them what they would like to achieve. Finding that the technique of getting his coachees to understand what they needed to do to improve rather than telling them was far more effective, he developed this into his 'Inner Game' theory. From this he developed the GROW model.

8.3 Feedback works both ways

> **Key technique:**
> - **Giving feedback**
>
> **Fundamental principle:**
> **Feedback can be given by anyone to anyone.**

What is feedback?

A common misconception exists that feedback is about a senior person telling off a junior one. Nothing could be further from the truth. Feedback is just as much about giving constructive praise as constructive criticism. And feedback can be given by any team member, no matter how junior or inexperienced. Feedback is a powerful technique that:

- gives people evidence-based observations about their behaviour that helps them to develop
- shows people that their development is recognised as being important
- builds trust between individuals who give and receive feedback.

Feedback is a conversation between two parties: a provider and a recipient. A conversation is started by either a provider offering feedback or a recipient asking for it – either party can refuse the offer or request. This is an important point which highlights the two-way nature of feedback: both parties have to be happy to take part in the conversation. Once both parties agree to taking part in a feedback conversation it can be provided in a variety of different forms – such as face-to-face, by email or by telephone. The conversation should follow the five-step process summarised in Figure 8.2.

When you give feedback, you should always abide by the three principles of great feedback:

1 Evidence-based – feedback must be grounded in evidence. 'I think your data analysis skills could be better' is neither an evidence-based nor a helpful piece of feedback; 'the discounted cash flow analysis you did last week had some hard-coding and incorrect formulae' is.

2 Private – feedback is a private conversation between the provider and the recipient. No-one else should know or hear about the feedback unless the recipient gives their consent.

3 Timely – feedback should be given as soon after the event as possible. The observation on which the feedback is based should be fresh in the minds of both provider and recipient.

How should you give feedback?

Just like setting up an interview (*Section 4.2*), when you decide to offer feedback to someone you should tell them of your intention beforehand. When you do, ask whether they would like to receive feedback; when would be convenient for them to receive it; and in what format they would like it. Feedback should be offered, not forced, so remember it is absolutely fine for someone to refuse feedback from you. They may have perfectly good reasons for not wanting to accept feedback: their mind might be on something else; they may not have time; or they may not see the value in receiving feedback from you. If the latter reason is the case, then it is their loss. By giving feedback to more receptive individuals in your organisation, you will gain a good reputation as someone who cares about the development of others. Soon anyone who originally refused your offer of feedback will be knocking on your door asking for some!

Because feedback doesn't have to be accepted by the proposed recipient, this makes it very different from direct praise or criticism. This is where the provider *tells* the recipient whether their performance has been good or bad. Whilst there is always a time and place for this kind of interaction, you should not confuse it with feedback. Feedback is a two-way conversation; direct praise or criticism is just a statement.

You don't need to be an expert on a given subject to give feedback. For example, it is perfectly reasonable for a junior person on a team to give a more senior person feedback (positive or critical) on their presentation or management style. Even if the junior person has never managed before, because they have experience of being managed they may have some useful feedback to give to their seniors. Similarly, whilst a junior may not have much experience in giving presentations, they may have experience of being presented to, and could give feedback on the clarity of a presentation or how it made them feel.

Figure 8.2 Feedback conversation process

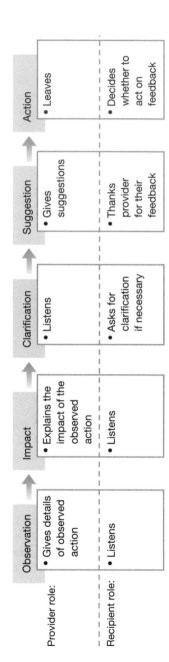

If you ask someone to give you feedback, give them forewarning about this and be specific about what you want them to focus on. For instance, if you want someone to give you feedback on your meeting facilitation technique, tell them something like:

'I'd really like your thoughts on my meeting facilitation technique. Next Tuesday I'm running the solutions generation brainstorming session with members of the finance team. As you'll be at the session, I was wondering if you could please watch out for how I facilitate the session, and in particular on how I get the quieter team members to engage in brainstorming. If you could give me some feedback on this over a coffee on Wednesday I'd be hugely grateful.'

Whoever gives feedback must make sure that the conversation between provider and recipient follows the five-step process summarised in Figure 8.2.

Observation
At the start of the conversation, the provider should tell the recipient what observations their feedback is based on. This should be evidence-based and specific. For example: 'When you were discussing the business plan with the Finance Director in yesterday's meeting you had a tendency to talk over him and your body language was rather confrontational.'

Impact
The provider should then explain what impact this observation had on them. By explaining the impact, the importance of the feedback becomes apparent. For instance: 'Your behaviour with the Finance Director made me concerned about your interpersonal skills and I am worried that as a result he will be less supportive of our work in future.'

Clarification
The provider should give the recipient an opportunity to seek clarification of the observations made. In this example the recipient might ask: 'In what way did my body language seem confrontational?', thereby requesting the provider to give more details of their observation.

Suggestion
In preparation for the feedback session, the provider should have thought of a series of suggestions to make to the recipient to help them improve on (or maintain, if the feedback is positive) the areas mentioned in the feedback. Continuing the example, the provider could suggest the recipient: watches their body language in future and avoids leaning in when talking to people; be more conscious about talking over people; or attends a people management training course.

Action
Once the provider has finished and the recipient has thanked them for their time, it is up to the recipient whether to act on the feedback and suggestions given. This is

a crucial point about feedback. Just as you can refuse to receive it, you can refuse to act on it too – it is up to the recipient. At the very least, the recipient should make a note of the feedback received so they can build up a picture of their strengths and weaknesses.

When should you give feedback?

Feedback can be offered or requested at any point in the problem-solving process, or in fact at any point in any process. However, when you get around to giving or receiving feedback, remember that it should be *private* and *timely* – you will need to set up an appropriate time for the feedback conversation to take place.

Who should give feedback?

Anyone can give feedback: team member or stakeholder, junior or senior, experienced or novice. All that matters is that the feedback they give is done in private, is evidence-based, timely and that the feedback conversation follows the five-step process summarised in Figure 8.2.

Example Josie has been working on a tough project bringing a new soft drink to market. One of her team members – Erik – has just delivered an interim presentation to stakeholders updating them on the team's progress. Josie wants to give Erik some feedback on his presentation style, and after the meeting is over she takes him to one side.

Josie: *Erik, good work giving the presentation today. I was wondering if you'd like some feedback on it.*

Erik: *Thanks, that would be really helpful. My day's looking pretty hectic right now but could you maybe give me the feedback over coffee tomorrow morning?*

Josie: *No problem, let's take a break around 10am tomorrow and we can have a 15-minute chat then.*
[Conversation the next day...]

Josie: *I thought you did a really solid job in the presentation yesterday. The messages were clear, you dealt with some tough questions well, and you made sure to look at everyone in the audience as you spoke. There was just one thing that stood out as a potential area for you to work on.*

Erik: *Thanks, I thought it went OK too. So what do you think I need to improve on?*

[Observation]

Josie: *Well, whilst you were presenting I thought your hands were quite restless. You seemed to be always gesticulating, but often not in a* way that related to the PowerPoint slides. I noticed your hands never seemed to settle in a resting position; they were sometimes in your pockets, other times they were held behind your back, and at one point it even looked a bit like you were praying.

Erik: Yes, I was a bit worried about that.

[Impact]

Josie: Don't worry, it's not a major problem, but I think the impact it has on people is to distract them a bit. At one point someone was staring at your hands rather than the slides, and I doubt he was paying too much attention to what you were saying then either.

[Clarification]

Erik: Did you notice me doing this at any particular points in the presentation?

Josie: It seemed to happen most frequently when there was quite a bit of information on a slide. I don't know if that made you nervous, but when there was only a small amount of text on a slide and what you were saying was the main focus of the presentation then your hands seemed a lot calmer. When there was loads of text or a complicated chart, then your gesticulations got a little bit frantic. Does that make sense?

Erik: Yes. I hadn't really thought about it before, but now that you mention it I think that's most probably true.

[Suggestion]

Josie: Don't let this worry you lots. As I said before, overall you did a good job, but this might be something you want to work on. One way to do this could be to carefully plan when you want to use your hands to articulate a point. You could highlight this in your speaker notes if you have some. Then when you're not using your hands, you could find a default position to keep them in. If there's a lectern, you could think about resting them on this. Or if there isn't anywhere to rest your hands, then some people find that having one arm resting by your side and other hand in the position of a gently clenched fist near your stomach looks quite relaxed. Alternatively, when you see other people give presentations, make a note of what looks good and try it out yourself. The key thing is that you're aware of the effect of your gesticulations: remember you want to look natural but in control.

Erik: Thanks, that's really helpful. I really appreciate you taking the time to give me this feedback.

Josie: You're welcome. Maybe some time you could give me some feedback on how I give presentations? I find it's always useful to get people's opinions.

Erik: Great – next time you present I'll make sure I do. Thanks again, Josie.

[Action]

After they have ended their conversation, Erik thinks about the feedback he has received. He hadn't worried much about his hands before, but he accepts that they were flailing around a bit during the presentation. He decides to act on Josie's feedback. Next time he presents, he'll think of a default position to keep his hands in (based on some videos of great presentations he plans to look up on the internet), and will make a mental note of when and how to use them based on the slides he presents. He appreciated Josie's request of feedback from him, and as a way of thanking her for taking the time to give him feedback, he resolves to offer her some feedback in the future.

Tips and tricks

- Be the feedback champion. Your organisation probably claims it has a great feedback culture (most do), but the reality may be very different. Often this is because people are afraid of upsetting people by giving feedback. Don't be afraid to offer and ask for feedback frequently. By giving it you will be making people aware of its benefits. By asking people you will show there is demand for it.

- You can never give too little feedback, but you can give too much. Feedback should be given often, though how frequently depends on individuals and organisational culture. Start by giving feedback to someone once a week and asking for it once a week too, changing the frequency later on as you see fit. If you give feedback multiple times a day to the same individual you can reduce its effectiveness. To avoid this, before giving feedback ask yourself: 'Would I find this feedback helpful?' This should help to stop you giving trivial feedback.

- It is possible to give feedback to groups of people. For example, the feedback provider could be a judging panel and the recipient could be a team of individuals. The principles of feedback should still be adhered to even though it is no longer a conversation between just two people.

- Mixing positive and development feedback into a conversation can be a useful way to avoid seeming overly critical or attacking of the recipient. However, make sure that any feedback you give isn't forced or trivial. Feedback should always be honest and helpful; if you find you want to say something positive just for the sake of it, it may be better to say nothing at all.

- Whilst you don't need to act on feedback you receive, you should have a good reason for not doing so. Remember that all feedback is valid. Even if you don't agree with it, the fact that you have been given feedback on something means that is how people perceive you or your actions.

Summary

- Feedback is a powerful technique where one individual gives another constructive criticism or praise. It is useful in:
  - developing people
  - making people know that their development is important
  - building trust.
- Anyone can give or receive feedback. All that matters is that the feedback is given in private, that it is timely, and crucially, that it is evidence-based.
- Feedback is a two-way conversation between a provider and a recipient. This process follows five steps:
  1 Provider makes an observation.
  2 Provider explains the impact of the observation.
  3 Recipient seeks clarification if necessary.
  4 Provider gives suggestions for improvement.
  5 Recipient decides whether to act on the feedback.
- Feedback is not about telling people off; it is about helping people develop. As such, feedback should be used to make positive as well as critical observations known to individuals, and help them to maintain or improve their performance accordingly.

Did you know?

The term *coaching* was first used to refer to an instructor as a form of slang in Oxford University in the mid-nineteenth century. Originally the term rather pejoratively referred to special training that a candidate would receive in order to help get them through an exam. Some years later it began to be used in a sporting sense.

End of manage the team checklist

Team management runs throughout the OBTAIN problem-solving process. During the process, you should have:
- **determined who is in the problem-solving team**
- **allocated the nine Belbin roles across the team**
- **helped team members develop through using the IT-GROW framework**
- **given and received feedback to and from all members of the team.**

A final thought

Congratulations on reaching the end of *Key business solutions*. Through successfully solving your problems using the OBTAIN process and keeping your stakeholders and team happy with the tools and techniques laid out in the text, you are sure to be on your way to becoming an expert problem-solver.

Before you put down this book and tell all your friends and colleagues about its benefits, one final thought. Far too often business feels like a never-ending race to get ahead; always forward-looking, desperate for progress. There is never any time to look back and reflect on the journey just taken. We rarely give ourselves the space in our working day (or even our non-working day) to learn from our past mistakes or even our triumphs. This is a big mistake and the reason why so often it seems that we never learn the lessons of history.

Every time you complete the OBTAIN process, or just one of its stages, or even just use one of its tools, make sure to spend time reflecting on the positives and negatives of the experience. Keep a note of these and devise a plan for building or improving on them. This can involve tailoring the tools or techniques to your preference, coming up with new methodologies yourself, or just learning more about yourself and how you cope under different circumstances. As the great statesman Winston Churchill once said, 'Those that fail to learn from history are doomed to repeat it.' Take heed of this sage advice. And I wish you great success in your future problem-solving endeavours.

[PART TWO]

Critical business tools and frameworks

Critical business tools and frameworks

9

The following tools and frameworks have been included in this book for two reasons. Firstly, because they are powerful tools which are commonly used to help solve business problems. And secondly, whilst they don't fit exactly into the OBTAIN process, they can be used to complement the different stages of the process, or as individual stand-alone techniques.

Table 9.1 shows where the critical business tools and frameworks can be used in the OBTAIN process.

4Ps of marketing

What is it?

The 4Ps of marketing (also known as the 'marketing mix') helps you understand how to position your market offer.

When should you use it?

The 4Ps is most commonly used when planning the strategy for bringing a product or service to market. However, it is not limited to this, and can be used in a variety of situations. For example, the framework can be used in an *issue tree,* when breaking down potential marketing analyses; in a *hypothesis tree,* when testing the current marketing strategy; or in framing the recommendations of a *final report.*

Table 9.1 Where to use them

	Outline	Breakdown	Test	Analyse	Imagine	Notify	Manage the team	Manage the stakeholders
4Ps of marketing	✓	✓	✓			✓		
5Cs	✓		✓	✓				
Ansoff matrix	✓		✓	✓				
BCG growth-share matrix				✓	✓			
Benchmarking	✓				✓			
Brainstorming	✓	✓	✓	✓	✓			
De Bono's six thinking hats			✓	✓	✓			
Drill-down analysis	✓		✓	✓				
Kano analysis							✓	✓
McClelland's theory of needs							✓	✓
McKinsey 7S framework			✓		✓	✓		
PESTEL		✓		✓				
SWOT	✓		✓	✓				
Value chain analysis		✓	✓	✓				

How does it work?

The marketing mix (see Figure 9.1) forces you to think about the different elements that need to be considered when offering your services to customers.

For each of the Ps, a set of decisions will need to be made about the marketing strategy. For example:

- Price – pricing strategy, seasonal variations, volume discounts, etc.
- Product – customer needs, branding, difference from competitors, etc.
- Place – vendors, need for a sales force, warehousing, etc.
- Promotion – advertising, timing of marketing campaigns, marketing budget, etc.

When making these decisions, you must always keep in mind your target audience. What do they want from the product? How can you best satisfy their needs?

Figure 9.1 The marketing mix

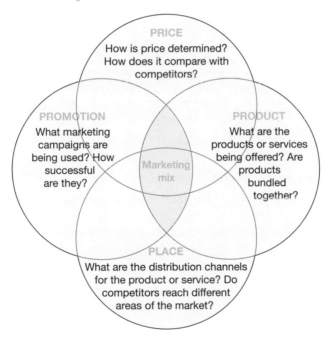

5Cs of strategy

What is it?

5Cs is a simple framework for conducting a strategic analysis of an organisation. By answering the questions posed in each of the sections, your answers will provide you with a detailed understanding of the issues facing an organisation.

When should you use it?

Any time you want to understand more about a particular organisation (either your own, a competitor, or one you may be looking to acquire), the 5Cs is a useful tool for your strategic analysis.

How does it work?

Thinking about each of the Cs covered in the framework, answer the questions posed in Table 9.2, and any more you may think relevant.

Table 9.2 Example questions relating to the 5Cs

5Cs	Example questions
Company	What is the company's turnover?
	What products or services does it provide?
	What are its strengths and weaknesses?
Competition	Who are the competitors?
	What market share do they hold?
	What strategic advantages do they hold?
Costs	What are the costs; are they fixed or variable?
	How do the costs compare with industry averages?
	What opportunities are there for reducing costs?
Customers	Who are the customers?
	What are the customer's needs? Are they being met?
	How can customer numbers be increased?
Channels	What are the distribution channels for the product or services offered?
	How can the distribution channels be increased?
	Which market areas remain untapped?

Use the answers from the 5Cs analysis to build a picture of the nature of the organisation you are interested in. This can complement your SWOT, 7S and PESTEL analyses.

Ansoff matrix

What is it?

The Ansoff matrix – developed by one of the leading thinkers in strategic management, Igor Ansoff – helps to identify corporate growth strategies for products or services.

The different growth quadrants described in the matrix provide a helpful way of thinking about growth strategies. This can be useful when testing hypotheses about new or existing growth strategies in *hypothesis trees* or when thinking about the types of analyses needed to understand the risks involved in a strategy plan.

How does it work?

Each of the quadrants in the matrix describes a different growth strategy which an organisation can choose based on its product offering and the markets in which it operates (see Figure 9.2).

Figure 9.2 Example Ansoff matrix

	Existing product	New product
New market	**Market development** Achieve growth through offering current products or services to new market	**Diversification** Achieve growth through new opportunities; both the product and market are new to the organisation
Existing market	**Market penetration** Increase market share through growth from current product offering and market segments	**Product development** Develop new products to replace or complement current offerings; target at existing market segments

Source: Adapted from 'Strategies of diversification', *Harvard Business Review*, 25(5), 113–25, Sept–Oct (Ansoff, I. 1957). Reproduced with permission.

Each of the strategies comes with different benefits and risks:

Market penetration

The least risky option as it requires no new products being developed or markets being entered. However, its success is dependent on the current market not being saturated. This strategy should be chosen only where there are prospects of growth in the market, competitors' market shares are falling, economies of scale are possible, and there is the possibility of selling more to existing customers.

Market development

A moderate risk option which involves maintaining existing products but entering into new markets. This strategy should be chosen where there are untapped markets, distribution channels to these markets are easily accessible, and the organisation has the capacity and capability to move into a new market.

Product development

A moderate risk option involves developing new products to offer to existing customers. New products can either replace, improve on or complement existing product offerings. This strategy should be selected when the organisation has the capacity to invest in developing new products, there is growth in the current market, and where the organisation has a strong brand identity that a new product can build on.

Diversification

This is the most risky strategy, where a new product is offered to a new market – two unknown areas for the company. There are two types of diversification: related (where the new markets and products share some characteristics with existing markets and products of the company) and unrelated (where the new markets and products are completely unknown to the company). Related diversification strategies can be sub-divided into three different forms:

- Horizontal diversification – completely new products to the organisation are offered to existing organisation markets.
- Vertical diversification – strategy focuses around tailoring new product offering to existing customers' needs.
- Concentric diversification – where new products that are similar to current product offerings are introduced to completely new markets.

There is one form of unrelated diversification:

- Conglomerate diversification – where a completely new form of product is offered to a new market; this is the highest-risk option.

BCG growth-share matrix

What is it?

Developed by Bruce Henderson of The Boston Consulting Group in the early 1970s, the BCG growth-share matrix is a simple but powerful tool that helps you plot the profit and growth potential of products or services in your organisation's portfolio.

When should you use it?

The growth-share matrix can be helpful when devising an organisation investment portfolio or in understanding how your product or service may be viewed by potential investors.

How does it work?

The two axes in the matrix are based on *market share* of the product or service relative to its competitors, and *rate of market growth* of the product or service (see Figure 9.3). Consistency and objectivity are essential to using the matrix effectively, so before you plot the matrix it is advisable to come up with a set of criteria for use. Thus 'high' market growth might be considered 8% real growth per annum, and 'low' relative market share might be something like a quarter the size of the market leader. Consistency and a decent grasp of the current market are key to ensuring sensible criteria which will make the analysis useful.

As critics have highlighted, though the matrix is very helpful in getting an overall sense of your organisation product portfolio, it is worth questioning and investigating further one of the basic assumptions of the matrix: that investment always leads to increase market growth or profitability. This is not always the case.

Figure 9.3 The BCG growth-share matrix

	High	Low
High	**Stars** Likely to be highly profitable with a good chance of increased growth. Investment recommended.	**Question marks** Growth rate uncertain. Additional investment could lead to high profitability, but not necessarily. Worth further investigation.
Low	**Cash cows** Highly profitable with little investment needed to maintain market share. The returns from cash cows should be used to keep the company growing and finance its investments.	**Dogs** If profitable, maintain but do not invest further. If not profitable, divest as soon as possible.

Market growth rate (vertical axis: High / Low)

Relative market share (horizontal axis: High / Low)

Source: Adapted from The BCG Portfolio Matrix from the Product Portfolio Matrix, © 1970, The Boston Consulting Group. Reproduced with permission.

Benchmarking

What is it?

The best performing organisations are those which continuously strive to be the best at what they do. Benchmarking allows you to understand where your organisation sits amongst its peers in terms of processes and performance.

When should you use it?

Benchmarking is useful in understanding the nature of your organisation; in setting realistic goals; and in generating ideas for solutions by looking to adopt industry best practice. You can also use benchmarking outside of an organisational setting; for instance, to understand how your own circumstances compare with others' when conducting your *work-life satisfaction assessment (Section 7.3)*.

How does it work?

Broadly speaking, there are four types of benchmarking (see Table 9.3). Each has its own benefits and is appropriate under different circumstances.

Table 9.3 Different types of benchmarking

Type	Aim	Benefits
Organisational	To compare performance between different parts of the same organisation.	Spreading good practice throughout the organisation; increasing awareness of different organisational practices; introducing a competitive element to organisation performance.
Performance	To compare operational performance with direct competitors.	Understanding competitor performance; learning from competitor good and bad practices; better awareness of what customers value.
Functional	To compare operational processes across the industry.	Understanding how to improve own internal processes by copying industry best practice.
External	To understand best practice processes from unrelated industries.	Gaining insight into best practice from unrelated industries can lead to creative thinking and innovative service improvements.

Once you have chosen what type of benchmarking you wish to undertake you should follow a four-step process:

1 Understand your organisation's own business processes that you wish to benchmark.
2 Collect the necessary data for the benchmarking.
3 Analyse the data to understand how your organisation compares to best practice.

4   Adopt best practice processes where appropriate to improve your
    performance.

Brainstorming

What is it?

Brainstorming is a process that encourages participants to come up with creative
and innovative ideas to solve problems. It should take place in a relaxed, informal
and non-judgemental session, where everyone is asked to come up with ideas for
dealing with a specific problem. The only rule that must be adhered to is that there
is no such thing as a bad idea in a brainstorming session. Even if an idea won't
solve the problem being discussed, it might help the rest of the team come up with
an idea that does.

When should you use it?

Brainstorming can be used throughout the OBTAIN process and is useful in many
business situations. Any time you find yourself stuck in similar ways of thinking,
or struggling to see the wood for the trees, a brainstorming session can help. By
encouraging creativity and innovation, brainstorming keeps people's minds fresh
and active. Through its non-hierarchical principle that everyone's ideas are equally
valid, brainstorming helps build team spirit. Brainstorming can also be conducted
individually; just try sketching out your ideas on a blank piece of paper and see
where they take you.

How does it work?

Brainstorming sessions should be relaxed, informal, and fun. Laying down strict
rules is a sure-fire way to inhibit the informality of the session, but here are some
guidelines to follow:

- Ensure the location for the session is comfortable and preferably different to
  the usual place of work.
- Provide fruit, healthy snacks and caffeine to keep energy levels up.
- Everyone should introduce themselves to the group.
- Use an ice-breaker to set a relaxed tone (see the example box below).
- Assign one person to be the ideas recorder for the session; they should
  write ideas up on a flip chart or whiteboard.
- Clearly explain the objective of the session; usually this will be to come up
  with ideas to solve a given problem.
- Ask everyone to come up with their own ideas individually first.
- As the ideas are read out and discussed by the rest of the group, ensure
  no-one is hostile or critical to a particular idea or person.

- Make sure only one person speaks at a time. If people are talking over others, warn the group that they will have to put their hands up to request to speak in future – this should stop the bad behaviour by drawing attention to it.
- Create a 'car park' that stores good ideas that are brought up during the session that don't quite fit with what is being currently discussed. Revisit these at the end of the session.
- Encourage and promote creativity. Suggest people think of completely different and unexpected industries to look for ideas. Asking left-field questions like 'How would a theme park deal with this problem?', 'How would a Martian view the issue?' or 'What would Donald Trump make of this?' gets people to think outside the box.
- Take appropriate breaks to keep up energy levels. Good brainstorming should be tiring, so don't force the participants to keep going if they are mentally drained.
- Once the session is finished assign someone to write up the notes of the meeting and to send them to the rest of the team for comment.

Example Ice-breakers

- Each person tells the group three 'facts' about themselves: two true and one a lie. The group has to guess the lie.
- Each person answers the question: 'If you could be any animal, what would you choose and why?'
- In silence, each person has to mime the month their birthday falls in until the group guesses what it is.

De Bono's six thinking hats

What is it?

Edward de Bono's six thinking hats are about forcing yourself (and your organisation) to think about a problem or solution in different ways.

When should you use it?

Use of the six thinking hats is typically most effective in a brainstorming or workshop environment. The idea is that each of the different coloured hats represents a different focus of enquiry about a particular problem or strategy. Thus firstly, you must decide what problem or strategy you wish to analyse. Once you have done this, you must then cycle through the different coloured 'hats' discussing the issue.

If done in a group, everyone should have the same 'hat' at the same time, and the group should cycle through the six different hats, offering contributions to the problem relevant to the character of the hat (see Table 9.4). If done individually, the hats should act as a reminder of the different questions that need to be asked when considering a strategy or solution.

How does it work?

Depending on what colour 'hat' the individual or group is currently wearing, discussions should focus around the characteristics of the colours.

Table 9.4 Six thinking hats characteristics

Hat	Character	Emphasis on...	Questions
White	Factual	data	What information do we have? What information are we missing? How confident can we be about our data?
Red	Emotional	feelings	What does our 'gut instinct' say? How do we feel about this? How committed are we to this?
Black	Cautious	downsides	What are the obstacles? What do we stand to lose? How realistic is this?
Yellow	Optimistic	upsides	How can we make this work? What are the positives? What are the opportunities?
Green	Creative	possibilities	Can we turn our thinking upside down? What new technologies can we make use of? What can we learn from other industries?
Blue	Process	managing	What is actually important? What are the conclusions? How do we move forward?

Source: Data from **www.debonothinkingsystems.com/tools/6hats.htm**

By ensuring that the six different 'hats' are listened to you guarantee that you have looked at the issue from all angles.

Drill-down analysis

What is it?

Drill-down analysis is the use of various analytical techniques to interpret quantitative data sources.

When should you use it?

As robust analysis is the bedrock of any successful problem-solving, drill-down techniques should be used throughout the OBTAIN process. However in particular, they are likely to be used during the creation of the Value-Context-Performance-Hypothesis (VCPH) pack and the analyse stage.

How does it work?

Drill-down analysis can take a variety of forms. Table 9.5 lists some of the most common types of this analysis, along with the functions needed for them in the most common data analysis package – Microsoft Excel.

Kano analysis

What is it?

Kano analysis – developed by Professor Noriaki Kano in the 1980s – provides a framework for understanding how to meet and exceed your customer expectations.

When should you use it?

Kano analysis is often used in manufacturing to understand which aspects of a product meet customer needs. However, it can also be useful in understanding how to meet and exceed stakeholder expectations (see *Chapter 7*) and development relationships expectations (see *Chapter 8*) in the OBTAIN process. By treating your team and stakeholders as *customers* of your management skills, the principles of Kano analysis can help you to ensure you always exceed expectations.

How does it work?

Kano analysis works from the principle that there are three types of customer reactions to your performance: delighted, satisfied, and dissatisfied (see Figure 9.4).

The theory states that your product offerings (or actions as a team manager, for example) can be plotted somewhere on the Kano matrix. You want to ensure that you always complete actions which are customer *dissatisfiers* and *satisfiers* – the absence of these will leave your customers displeased with your offering. For instance, in a development relationship, your coachee might rate 'attending development relationship conversations' as a *dissatisfier*, and 'helping me think through

Table 9.5 Most common types of drill-down analysis

Type	Technique	Purpose	Function in Microsoft Excel
Basic	Addition	To add different numbers together.	+
	Division	To divide one number by another.	/
	Subtraction	To take one number away from another.	–
	Multiplication	To multiply one number by another.	*
Average	Mean	To find the sum of all values in a data set divided by the total number of values in the data set.	AVERAGE
	Median	To find the middle value in a data set ordered in ascending numerical value	MEDIAN
	Mode	To find the most commonly occurring value in a data set.	MODE
Variation	Minimum	To find the minimum value in a data set.	MIN
	Maximum	To find the maximum value in a data set.	MAX
	Standard deviation	To find the variation from the mean of a data set. A high standard deviation indicates that the data is spread across a large range of values; a low standard deviation indicates a tight distribution of values around the mean.	STDEV
Finance	Compound annual growth rate	To calculate the average rate of growth of a variable over a given period of time (i.e. weeks, months, years, etc.)	RATE
	Net present value	To calculate the future value of an option based on a given discount rate.	NPV
Statistics	Correlation	To ascertain the degree of relationship between two variables.	CORREL
	Confidence interval	To understand the reliability of an estimate based on a data set.	CONFIDENCE
	Quartile	To find the value at the 25th, 50th, and 75th percentile in a data set arranged in ascending numerical value.	QUARTILE

Figure 9.4 Kano analysis: customer reactions

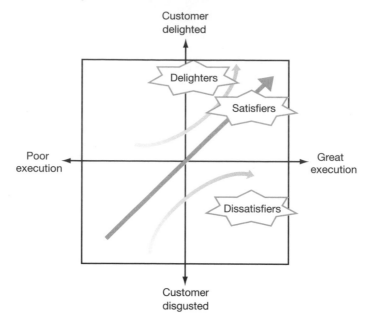

Source: Adapted from 'Attractive quality and must-be quality', *Hinshitsu: The Journal of the Japanese Society for Quality Control*, April, 39–48 (Kano, N., Seraku, N. Takahashi, F. and Tsuji, S. 1984). Reproduced with permission.

my goals' as a *satisfier*. If you failed to fulfil these actions your coachee would be highly displeased with your role as a coach; however, in fulfilling them you are unlikely to exceed your coachee's expectations. A coachee might consider 'taking time to fit in extra development conversations with me whenever I need them' as a *delighter* action. The coachee wouldn't expect this from you, but if you did this they would be delighted. You need to understand what these *delighters* are in your relationships with your stakeholders and team. Gathering data on this is difficult – sometimes you can obtain it through asking your customers (in this case your team or stakeholders), but this might not always be appropriate. Often you may just need to go on gut instinct. However, if you can identify and achieve these *delighters*, you will always exceed people's expectations of you – a very good thing.

McClelland's theory of needs

What is it?

The American psychologist David McClelland proposed that human beings are motivated (with variations in emphasis from individual to individual) by three basic needs: achievement, affiliation and power.

Table 9.6

High need for...	Characteristics	Working styles	Management tips
Achievement	Strives to be the best. Sets challenging but realistic goals. Dislikes unrealistic goals as they do not feel in control of them.	Likes to work alone or with other high achievement preference individuals.	Provide feedback to help them monitor progress towards their goals.
Affiliation	Need for acceptance and good relationships with others. Dislikes conflict.	Likes to work in teams with a high sense of cooperation.	Can risk being objective for the need to feel liked. Work to assuage any fears they may have about upsetting the sensitivities of team members – these fears will usually be without foundation.
Power	This can be either personal power (power over others) or institutional power (having organisational responsibilities).	Those with personal power preferences like to direct others; those with institutional power preferences like to organise others and harness the energies of the team.	Personal power preferences can be disruptive to team dynamics and need to be managed carefully – be explicit about what behaviour is acceptable in the workplace and the consequences of disregarding this. Institutional power preference can be harnessed to good organisational effect – keep an eye on it though, as unchecked it can lead to an overbearing desire to control things.

When managing individuals (see *Chapter 8* for more on this), McClelland's tripartite division of needs provides a useful framework for thinking about actions that can help improve motivation, and therefore job fulfilment and effectiveness. McClelland developed a Thematic Apperception Test (TAT) to understand in greater detail the extent of the preferences of each individual towards his three defined needs. Though TAT is still commonly used today for psychological research it is not without its detractors. It is therefore helpful to use McClelland's three needs more as a framework for thinking about motivational techniques, rather than as a strict theory that must be adhered to.

How does it work?

According to McClelland, depending on the strength of your preference for each need your motivational characteristics can be described as shown in Table 9.6.

McClelland's needs are not, of course, mutually exclusive. However, by understanding different emphasis on the three needs that individuals have, McClelland's divisions can provide a helpful way of thinking about team motivation.

McKinsey 7S framework

What is it?

The 7S framework – developed by McKinsey & Company consultants Waters, Peters and Philips in the 1980s – provides a way of ensuring that all the elements that make a successful company are aligned. This ensures a wholesome, comprehensive strategy, where all the factors that make successful companies reinforce and support each other.

When should you use it?

The framework can be used in a variety of manners. Most commonly, it is used to form a checklist of elements to consider when implementing change in an organisation. For example, if you are thinking of changing the composition of your workforce (i.e. affecting the 'staff' element) you should ask yourself: 'What impact will this have on the other six elements of the framework?' The interrelatedness of the 7S framework helps you to understand the knock-on effects which your changes may have.

In the OBTAIN process, you could consider using the McKinsey 7S framework when breaking down the problem in an *issue tree*, when testing your strategy using a *hypothesis tree*, or when thinking about the impact of implementing your solution.

How does it work?

The 7S framework divides the seven organisation elements of successful companies into two categories: 'hard' – tangible, easy to identify and manage; and 'soft' – intangible, often neglected, but just as important as the 'hard' factors. These are summarised in Figure 9.5.

Figure 9.5 The hard and soft elements

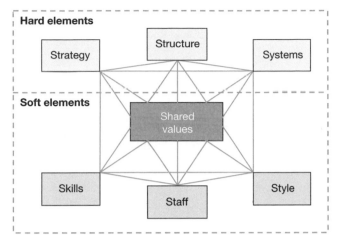

Source: Adapted from 'Structure is not organization', Mckinsey Quarterly (Waterman, R.H., Peters, T.J. and Phillips, J.R. 1980). Reproduced with permission.

These elements are defined as:

- strategy – the company's set goals and plan for achieving them
- structure – the organisational structure and hierarchical divisions
- systems – the procedures and processes used in the day-to-day working of the company
- style – the leadership style exhibited throughout the organisation
- staff – the people who work for the organisation
- skills – the capabilities of the organisation that are formed from the six other elements (not just the staff)
- shared values – the corporate culture; the beliefs and expectations that people have of the company.

PESTEL

What is it?

The PESTEL tool provides a framework for understanding the changes within the macro-environment that your organisation operates in.

When should you use it?

It is at this early stage of the problem-solving process that you want to be laying the foundations of your understanding of the problem at hand – this is when you should aim to use the PESTEL tool.

How does it work?

A PESTEL analysis considers the impact of potential changes to the operating environment of a company. The analysis looks at six broad areas and considers:

- How likely are these factors to change?
- How important are these factors to the company?

PESTEL is an acronym for the six factors to consider which are:

Factor	Example issues
Political	i.e. government policy, such as investment in infrastructure
Economic	i.e. interest rates, taxation levels, inflation, economic growth, etc.
Social	i.e. changing trends, such as moves to healthier lifestyles
Technological	i.e. new products or ways of conducting business, such as online shopping
Environmental	i.e. need to meet carbon emissions targets
Legal	i.e. retirement age, health and safety, copyright issues

By identifying the key issues that are likely to affect your organisation in the future, you will have a better sense of the context within which you need to generate the solution to the problem at hand.

Porter's five forces

What is it?

In his book *Competitive Strategy* (1980) the world-renowned business strategist Michael Porter identified five forces which determine the competitiveness of an industry.

When should you use it?

An organisation should look to use Porter's five forces when either:

- it is looking to enter into a new industry or
- it wishes to understand its current position within an industry.

How does it work?

By identifying five distinct forces which affect the dynamics of a given industry, you should analyse your own organisation's current and/or future performance relative to the forces (depending on your situation). The five forces are shown in Figure 9.6.

Figure 9.6 Porter's five forces

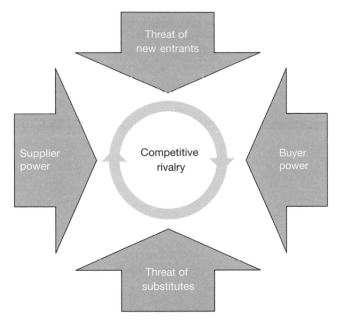

Source: Adapted from 'How competitive forces shape strategy', *Harvard Business Review*, March/April (Porter, M. 1979). Reproduced with permission.

For each of these forces, you must ask yourself a series of questions:

- Threat of new entrants – how is easy is it for new competitors to enter into the market?
- Threat of substitutes – how simple would it be for your offering to be replaced by something similar?
- Buyer power – what is the bargaining power of buyers? For example, how many of them are there? How much information do they have? In what volume do they buy?
- Supplier power – what impact do suppliers have on the industry? For example, how many of them are there? How much would it cost to switch supplier?
- Competitive rivalry – what existing advantages do competitors have? For example, how many competitors are there? How loyal are their customers? What are their brand reputations?

SWOT

What is it?

SWOT analysis provides a very simple framework for thinking about some key issues facing an organisation and the industry within which it operates.

When should you use it?

It is important to conduct SWOT analysis early on because this is when the foundations are set for the problem-solving process. If you leave this analysis until late on in the process it is easier to lose sight of the current state and fill your SWOT analysis with hypotheses and future-state suppositions. SWOT analysis can be helpful in filling out the *problem statement*, particularly in understanding the context behind a problem.

How does it work?

A SWOT analysis is driven by four questions that consider the internal and external health of an organisation (see Figure 9.7):

- What are the current internal **strengths** of the organisation? For instance: a particular expertise; a respected brand name; large existing customer base.
- What are the current internal **weaknesses** of the organisation? For instance: a lack of obvious expertise; weak brand identity; small existing customer base.
- What future external **opportunities** are there for the organisation? For instance: new markets in developing countries; increasingly affluent target demographic; recent competitor failures.
- What future external **threats** are there facing the organisation? For instance: market saturation; reduced customer purchasing power; regulatory changes.

Figure 9.7 A SWOT analysis

Strengths	Weaknesses
Opportunities	Threats

Key:
- Internal
- Current

- External
- Future

Whilst a SWOT analysis can be hugely effective in its simplicity, there are a few key points to remember when using it:

- Be as evidence-based and as specific as possible – SWOT analyses are highly subjective by nature.
- Keep in mind that you are dealing with your organisation *today*, not under some future hypothetical scenario.
- Remember that not all issues in your SWOT are equally important – try to rank and prioritise where appropriate.

Value chain analysis

What is it?

Porter's value chain analysis – from his 1985 book *Competitive Advantage* – divides the performance of a company into 'primary' and 'support' activities. This is based on the belief that by breaking down the different activities of a company and assessing performance for each of them, it is possible to see where the real strengths and weaknesses of a company lie.

When should you use it?

Value chain analysis is used primarily to understand what (if any) are the competitive advantages of a company – in other words, what it is better at than its competitors. By understanding this, it may be possible to devise a company strategy that maximises value through focusing on activities where it has a competitive value, and minimising cost by discarding or outsourcing those activities which are of minimum value.

How does it work?

Porter identifies nine different elements of the value chain which are split into two groups:

Primary activities

- Inbound logistics – receiving, storing and grouping the necessary inputs to create the product or service in the value chain.
- Operations – where the inputs are processed and transformed into the final product or service.
- Outbound logistics – the storage and then distribution of the finished product or service.
- Marketing and sales – any activities that encourage the purchase of the product or service by a potential buyer (i.e. advertising, promotion, selling, etc.).
- Service – the support to customers once they have purchased the product or service.

Support activities

- Firm infrastructure – including such factors as the organisation structure and accounting systems used by the organisation.
- Human resource management – recruitment, training, retention, salaries, etc.
- Technological development – such as research and development, product improvement, etc.
- Procurement – including purchasing, servicing and supplying the inputs needed for the product or service.

The aim is for all the activities in the value chain to give the final customer a level of value that is greater than the cost of each activity. If this is the case then a healthy profit margin will ensue.

However, few organisations will be excellent at all of the activities in the value chain. By breaking down what the different elements in the value chain are and by analysing the strengths and deficiencies of an organisation against each element you can gain insights into what an organisation excels at. In knowing this it is possible to focus on an organisational strategy that builds on the 'competitive advantages' (what the organisation is excellent at in the value chain) of the organisation.

Appendix: How the tools and techniques fit into the OBTAIN process

Sections and chapters	Tools and techniques covered
1. Outline the problem	
1.1 The problem may be big, but it should fit on one page	Problem statement
1.2 The key issues you need to know to solve the problem	Value-Context-Performance-Hypotheses (VCPH) pack
2. Break down the issues	
2.1 Untangling the mess	Issue tree
2.2 Prioritise your workload to maximise your effort: output ratio	2 × 2 prioritisation matrix Workplan
3. Test the hypothesis	
3.1 You are the doctor, the problem is your patient	Hypothesis tree
4. Analyse the problem	
4.1 Without data you have nothing	Data gathering
4.2 Insightful interviewing	Interviewing
4.3 If you want to get to the root cause of the problem, just ask 'why?'	5 whys
4.4 Making spreadsheet models easy	Spreadsheet modelling
5. Imagine the solution	
5.1 Devising the optimal solution	Arrange-Brainstorm-Choose (ABC) solutions generation process
5.2 Making change happen	Incentive equilibrium model
6. Notify the stakeholders	
6.1 Writing compelling reports	Report writing
6.2 Making great presentations	Creating presentations

Sections and chapters	Tools and techniques covered
7. Managing the stakeholders	
7.1 Understand who your stakeholders are and how to communicate with them	Stakeholder communication
7.2 Trust makes the world go around	Trust process
7.3 You are the most important stakeholder	Work-life satisfaction assessment
8. Managing the team	
8.1 Setting up the team to ensure success	Belbin team profiles
8.2 Helping others reach their goal	IT-GROW framework
8.3 Feedback works both ways	Giving feedback
9. Critical business tools and frameworks	
Quick reference guide to some of the key business tools which complement the OBTAIN process	4Ps of marketing; 5Cs; Ansoff matrix; BCG growth-share matrix; benchmarking; brainstorming; De Bono's six thinking hats; drill-down analysis; Kano analysis; McClelland's theory of needs; McKinsey 7S framework; PESTEL; Porter's five forces; SWOT; value chain analysis

Further reading and references

Business literature

Analysing data
For a useful introduction to Microsoft Excel and its functions, try: *Spreadsheet Projects in Excel for Advanced Level*, Julian Mott and Ian Rendell (2003). Oxford: Hodder Murray.

Benchmarking
The most authoritative text on the subject is: *Strategic Benchmarking: How to Rate Your Company's Performance against the World's Best*, G.H. Watson (1993). New York: John Wiley & Sons.

Change management
For an excellent overview, try: *Financial Times Briefing: Change Management*, Richard Newton (2010). Harlow: Financial Times Prentice Hall.

Coaching
One of the seminal works on coaching: *The Tao of Coaching*, Max Landsberg (2003, revised edition). London: Profile Books.

Communication skills
For a great synthesis on general communication techniques, try: *Improve Your Communication Skills*, Alan Barker (2010). London: Kogan Page.

Kano analysis
For more on Professor Kano's thoughts and insights on management techniques, see: *Continuous Improvement: Quality Control Circles in Japanese Industry*, Paul Lillrank and Noriaki Kano (1989). Ann Arbor, University of Michigan: Center for Japanese Studies.

Problem-solving
For an excellent free resource on problem-solving techniques and how they fit into the project management process, see the *2020 Delivery Project Primer* at **www.2020delivery.com**.

Team management
For more detail on Belbin team roles see: *Management Teams: Why They Succeed or Fail*, Meredith Belbin (1985). London: Heinemann. For more on David McClelland's work see *The Achieving Society* (1961). London: Free Press.

Stakeholder management

One of the world's leading thinkers on management has some fascinating thoughts on stakeholders in: *Managing*, Henry Mintzberg (2009). Harlow: Pearson Education. For more on trust and how to gain it, look at: *The Trusted Advisor*, David Maister *et al.* (2000). London: Simon & Schuster.

Strategy

The McKinsey 7S framework was originally expounded in: *The Art of Japanese Management*, Richard Pascale and Anthony Athos (1981). New York: Simon and Schuster. For more on Michael E. Porter's seminal Five Forces model, see *Competitive Strategy* (1980). New York: Free Press. Porter's value chain analysis is elaborated on in *Competitive Advantage: Creating and sustaining superior performance* (1998). New York: The Free Press. More detail on the Ansoff matrix is in: *Corporate Strategy*, Igor Ansoff (1970, revised edition). London: Penguin Books. Edward de Bono's *6 Thinking Hats* (1985) describes its eponymous strategy tool. London: Little, Brown. Bruce Henderson's BCG growth-share matrix was first described in *The Product Portfolio Matrix* (1970). BCG Perspectives, available on the BCG website: **www.bcg.com**. For a very useful summary of general strategic tools in business see: *Key Management Models*, Steven ten Have *et al.* (2003). London: Pearson Education. And *Key Management Models*, *2nd edition*, Marcel van Assen *et al.* (2009). London: Pearson Education.

Work-life balance

For more detail on how to achieve a work-life balance see: *Managing Work-Life Balance*, David Clutterbuck (2003). London: Chartered Institute of Professional Development. For tips on time management and increasing your effectiveness at work, see: *The 7 Habits of Highly Effective People*, S.R. Covey (1999). London: Simon and Schuster.

Writing skills

One of the key texts on writing technique in business is: *The Pyramid Principle*, Barbara Minto (2001, revised edition). Harlow: Financial Times Prentice Hall.

Did you know?

For more on the history of management consultancy (Did you know? from *Section 1.2*), see Chris McKenna's excellent overview of the industry in *The World's Newest Profession* (Cambridge: Cambridge University Press, 2006). Descartes' maxim *cogito ergo sum* (*Section 2.2*) was first pronounced – in Latin anyway – in *Principles of Philosophy* (New York: E. Mellen Press, 1988 [originally published 1644]). For a richly detailed history of management in Britain see Edward Brech's magnum opus, *The Evolution of Modern Management* (Bristol: Thoemmes, 2002). An excellent history of the computer and the state (*Section 4.4*) can be found in Jon Agar's *The Government Machine: A Revolutionary History of the Computer* (Cambridge, Mass:

MIT Press, 2003). An entertaining exploration of the theory of the wisdom of crowds (*Section 5.1*) can be found in James Surowiecki's *The Wisdom of Crowds* (London: Abacus, 2004). George Pólya's landmark text on problem-solving (*Section 5.2*) has been reissued: *How to Solve It: A New Aspect of Mathematical Method* (Oxford: Princeton University Press, 2004). For Edward Tufte's critique of PowerPoint (*Section 6.2*), read his tract *The Cognitive Style of PowerPoint* (Graphic Press, 2003). Socrates' discussion of trust with Plato's brother (*Section 7.2*), Glaucon, is in *Republic* (Oxford: Oxford University Press, 2008). More on the growth of consumerism in the twentieth century (*Section 7.3*) is in Avner Offer's *The Challenge of Affluence* (Oxford: Oxford University Press, 2006). The Hawthorne Effect is described in more detail in Richard Gillespie's *Manufacturing Knowledge: A History of the Hawthorne Experiments* (Cambridge: Cambridge University Press, 1991). For more on Timothy Gallwey's Inner Game theory (*Section 8.3*) see *The Inner Game of Work* (New York: Random House, 2000). Finally, for the etymological descriptions of *data* (*Section 4.2*), *computer* (*Section 4.4*), *stakeholder* (*Section 7.1*) and *coaching* (*Section 8.3*) refer to the *Oxford English Dictionary*.

Index

drill-down analysis 64–6, 180, 181

E-Z Learn 16–19
end products 5, 7, 10
enunciation 113
environmental groups 119
error reduction programmes 87–9
evaluation criteria 75, 77–8, 81
evidence-based arguments 108
evidence-based feedback 159
executive summary 98, 99
expectations of stakeholders 130–1
expert advice 19
external benchmarking 176
eye contact 113

feedback 158–65
    action 161–2, 164
    clarification 161, 163
    conversation process 159–64
    evidence-based 159
    how to give 159
    impact 161, 163
    observation 161, 162–3
    private 159
    suggestion 161, 163
    timely 159
    too little/too much 164
    when to give 162
final presentations 114, 115
final reports 103–4
financial rewards 85, 86, 89
findings of reports 98, 100
finishers 147
firm infrastructure 189
5 whys 61–4
5Cs of strategy 171–2
five forces analysis 186–7
flip charts 63
focus 28
font styles 107
football club 31–5
Ford, Henry 29
format of data 54
formatting reports 102
4Ps of marketing 28, 169–71
friendly stakeholders 120, 121
front page of reports 98, 99
functional benchmarking 176
fundraising 77–9

Galton, Sir Francis 84
gap-analysis 157
Gaskins, Robert 116
gestures 113
Glass-Steagal Act (1933) 20
Glaucon 135
goals 4, 74–5, 77
    of interviews 55

IT-GROW framework 151–8
    SMART goals 6, 154, 156
grammar 105
great presentations 106
group solutions 77
GROW model 158
growth-share matrix 174–5
grumbling stakeholders 120, 121
gut feelings 48
Gyges 135
gym chain 149–50

Hammond, Henry 54
hard coding models 68
Hawthorne Effect 151
Highbrowse 42–4
honourability 129, 132–3
horizontal diversification 174
human resource management 190
hypothesis testing 41
hypothesis tree 38–45, 76, 108
    definition 38
    initial hypothesis 12–20, 38
    invalid hypothesis 41
    output from interviews 57
    process of hypothesising 41
    qualitative information 41
    quantitative information 41
    refining 45
    when to use 41–2

ice-breakers 178
ideas see brainstorming
identifying stakeholders119 123
Imagine stage 73–91
    change management 84–91
    optimal solution 74–84
impact 161, 163
implementation 76, 86–7, 89, 98, 101
implementers 147
incentive equilibrium model 84–91
incentivisation 51, 85–6
inductive reasoning 95–7, 107
influence of stakeholders 119, 120
initial hypothesis 12–20, 38
input data 66
intention 153, 156
interim presentations 72, 114, 115
interim reports 75, 103
interviews 51, 53, 55–61
    agenda 55–6
    body language 56, 60
    closed questions 60
    definition 55
    during stage 56, 60
    goals 55
    issue trees 55
    listening skills 56
    location 60

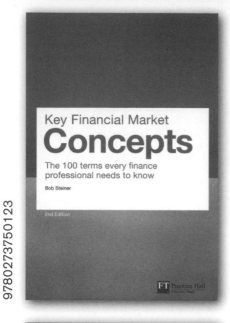

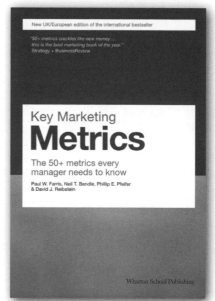